INSIDE THE ANCIENT

ROMAN PROVINCIAL
ADMINISTRATION
227 BC to AD 117

INSIDE THE ANCIENT WORLD

General Editor: M. R. F. Gunningham

Other titles in the series

INSIDE THE ANCIENT WORLD

ROMAN PROVINCIAL ADMINISTRATION
227 BC to AD 117

JOHN RICHARDSON

MACMILLAN EDUCATION

First published 1976
Reprinted 1978

Published by
MACMILLAN EDUCATION LTD
*Houndmills Basingstoke Hampshire RG21 2XS
and London
Associated companies in Delhi Dublin
Hong Kong Johannesburg Lagos Melbourne
New York Singapore and Tokyo*

Printed in Hong Kong

Contents

Illustrations

Maps

Acknowledgements

The author and publishers wish to thank the following photograph sources:

Cover: Prof. W. A. J. Watson, University of Edinburgh.
British Museum pp. 63, 74; Gabinetto Fotografico p. 22; Fototeca Unione pp. 50, 53, 66; German Archaeological Institute p. 60; Glyptotek, Copenhagen p. 19 bottom right and left; A. F. Kersting p. 76; Kunsthistorisches Museum p. 81; Mansell Collection p. 36; Leonard Von Matt p. 19 top.

The author wishes to acknowledge the assistance of the University of St Andrews, who have made a grant towards the cost of researching this book.

General Editor's Preface

To get *inside* the Ancient World is no easy task. What is easy is to idealise the Greeks and Romans, or else to endow them unconsciously with our own conventional beliefs and prejudices. The aim of this series is to illuminate selected aspects of antiquity in such a way as to encourage the reader to form his own judgement, from the inside, on the ways of life, culture and attitudes that characterised the Greco-Roman world. Where suitable, the books draw widely on the writings (freshly translated) of ancient authors in order to convey information and to illustrate contemporary views.

The topics in the series have been chosen both for their intrinsic interest and because of their central importance for the student who wishes to see the civilisations of Greece and Rome in perspective. The close interaction of literature, art, thought and institutions reveals the Ancient World in its totality. The opportunity should thus arise for making comparisons not only within that world, between Athens and Sparta, or Athens and Rome, but also between the world of antiquity and our own.

The title 'Classical Studies' (or 'Classical Civilisation') is featuring more and more frequently in school timetables and in the prospectuses of universities. In schools, the subject is now examined at Advanced Level as well as at sixteen plus (O Level and CSE), and it is chiefly for such courses that this new series has been designed. It is also intended as a helpful ancillary to the study of Latin and Greek in the sixth form and below and many of the books will be found particularly useful by those candidates working towards the *Cambridge Latin Course* examination. It is hoped that some topics in the series will interest students of English and History at these levels as well as the non-specialist reader.

The authors, who are teachers in schools or universities, have each taken an aspect of the Ancient World. They have tried not to give a romanticised picture but to portray, as vividly as possible, the Greeks and the Romans as they really were.

It is sometimes forgotten just how vast, in terms of both time and geographical extent, the Roman empire was. An area covering, roughly speaking, from the Atlantic to the Caucasus and from Scotland to the Sahara was held by the Romans for about four hundred and fifty years. The very existence of such an empire was Rome's greatest achievement, and it was the result of her dominance that led to the impact of Greco-Roman ideas, institutions and literature on Western civilisation.

In this book Dr Richardson shows how this empire emerged and how the Romans set about governing the great areas under their control in the formative period from Rome's first acquisition of provinces after the First Punic War down to the beginning of the second century AD. The example of Rome's government of her provinces shows clearly that one state cannot control the destiny of others without this making great differences not only to those controlled but also to the ruling power. In tracing these changes in the outlook of the men who governed Rome's provinces and in the institutions they used for the purpose, the author sheds light not only on Rome and Roman civilisation, but on the age-old question of the methods and the justification of world power.

July 1975   MICHAEL GUNNINGHAM

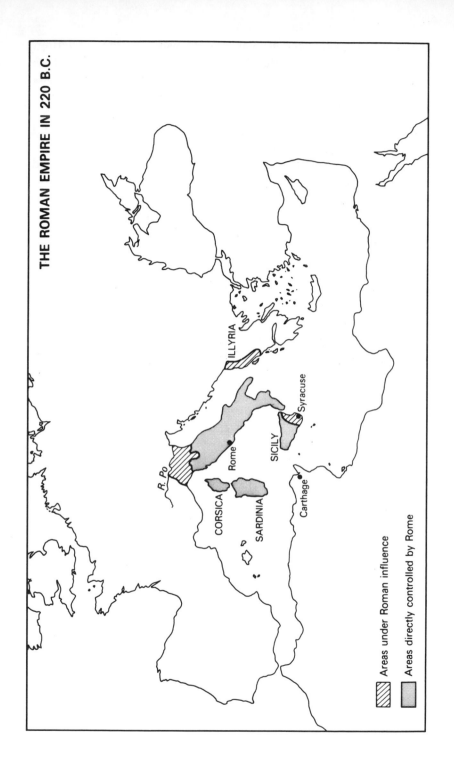

THE ROMAN EMPIRE IN 220 B.C.

ILLYRIA

R. Po

Rome

CORSICA

SARDINIA

SICILY

Syracuse

Carthage

Areas under Roman influence

Areas directly controlled by Rome

I
Rome and her empire

THE Romans had an empire long before they had an emperor. By the time the Roman republic had come to an end, and Augustus was firmly established as the first of the emperors in 28 BC, Roman governors had been in Sardinia and parts of Sicily for two hundred years. By far the greater part of the area which the emperors were to rule for the next four centuries had been administered first by men sent from Rome by the republican senate. As we shall see, in a real sense it was the fact that Rome had an empire to control that was to lead to the need for one strong man to rule it – the empire produced the emperor. But how did Rome come to control an empire?

Rome becomes a Mediterranean power

> For who is so worthless or so lazy that he does not wish to know by what means and under what form of government almost the entire inhabited world fell under the control of one empire, that of the Romans, in a period of not quite fifty-three years?
>
> [Polybius, I 1.5]

With these words the Greek historian Polybius, writing in about 150 BC, urged the educated men of Greece to read his history of the rise of Rome to supreme power in the Mediterranean world. He was speaking of the period from 219 BC, just before the outbreak of the great war between Rome and the Carthaginian general Hannibal, and 167 BC when the Roman army finally overthrew the kingdom of Macedonia, which for over a century and a half had dominated the Greek states.

ROME AGAINST CARTHAGE

In fact the emergence of Roman power had already begun before the period Polybius mentions. When Rome first came into open conflict with Carthage in Sicily in 264, she was already the leader of a federation of states which covered the whole of the Italian peninsula south of the River Po. By the outbreak of the Second Punic War in 218, she controlled directly most of Sicily and the two islands of Sardinia and Corsica, all former Carthaginian possessions. These areas were not included within the Italian federation, but were, at least from 227 onwards, ruled by Roman governors. They formed the first of the long list of Rome's provinces overseas, and the beginnings of her Mediterranean empire.

The first great test of Rome's power in the western Mediterranean came in the long war between herself and Carthage between 218 and 202. Carthage had been the most important city in the whole area for nearly three hundred years, and though weakened as a result of her earlier defeat by the Romans she was still a force to be reckoned with. Rome's victory over the Carthaginian general Hannibal meant an increase in her territorial holdings. By 202 not only had she taken over the rest of Sicily, but she had also stationed troops along the eastern coast of Spain and in the rich areas of southern Spain, which had been a major battleground during the war against Hannibal, and before that a source of Carthaginian wealth.

AFTER THE WAR WITH HANNIBAL

However, once Rome was securely established as a great power in the ancient world, she seemed strangely uninterested in increasing her territorial empire. Wars in Spain slowly enlarged the area of the peninsula under her control, but there were no additions to her provinces elsewhere. Carthage remained an independent state, though her final peace with Rome greatly reduced her strength. In the early years of the second century BC Romans fought in Greece and in Asia Minor, and rival kings of far-away Egypt even appealed to the Roman senate to decide between them; but for over fifty years there was no expansion of the newly-won empire.

The reasons for this lull in the first half of the second century are complex, but one factor is worth noticing here. To the Romans, the governing of a province meant keeping troops there, and experience in Spain showed that this could mean a considerable number of soldiers being far from their Italian homes for several years at a time. This, together with the fact that the army and people of Rome had just finished a desperate war against Carthage, almost certainly made the senate unwilling to take on long-term commitments overseas and thus to acquire new provinces. Instead the senate preferred to influence events in the Mediterranean through diplomacy and, though quite prepared to use force, to restrict military operations to a series of fairly short campaigns.

In about 150 BC the storm broke. Over the next few years Rome, exasperated by what seemed to her the insolent refusal of Carthage and of Greece to toe the Roman line, sent in the legions. In 146 BC two of the great cities of the ancient world were sacked by Roman troops, her old enemy Carthage, and Corinth, the centre of Greek resistance to Roman demands. This time there were no half-measures. Henceforth Greece was to be under direct Roman control, and it was eventually divided into three provinces, Macedonia in the north, Achaea in the south and Epirus on the Adriatic coast facing Italy; Carthage and the area surrounding it became the Roman province of Africa. Even now, however, the senate was clearly unwilling to annex territory simply for the sake of increasing the size of the empire. For many years the southern part of Greece was not divided into provinces, and a watch was kept over this area by the Roman governor in Macedonia. Similarly, only a small area of the north African coast immediately around Carthage was annexed to form the province of Africa.

THE CLIENT KINGDOMS

This did not mean that Rome was restricting her influence over the Mediterranean to these relatively small and scattered areas. In many places she preferred to continue, as she had in the early second century, to use rulers who were already established, and to give support to them against enemies both inside and outside their kingdoms. Although both the senate and the client kings, as these rulers were called, could occasionally act in bad faith, ignoring their mutual agreements for their own ends, the scheme had many advantages. On the Roman side, the senate could exert its influence without the need to station troops overseas on a permanent basis. Moreover the representative of Rome in the area was a local ruler, much more used to the particular local situation than any governor from Rome. The client king had the security of Roman power to back him, so long as he followed Roman policy and Roman interests. Usually the senate was only too happy to allow him to rule the internal affairs of his country as he saw fit, provided that they themselves were not involved. Finally the local population of

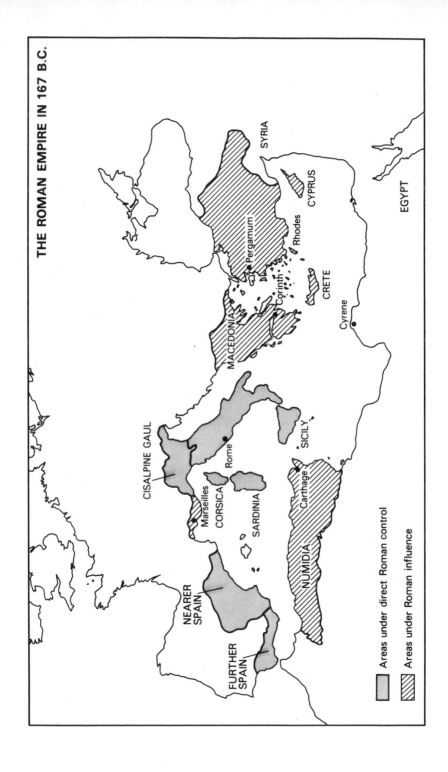

THE ROMAN EMPIRE IN 167 B.C.

SYRIA

CYPRUS

EGYPT

Pergamum

Rhodes

CRETE

Corinth

Cyrene

MACEDONIA

CISALPINE GAUL

Rome

SICILY

Marseilles

CORSICA

Carthage

SARDINIA

NUMIDIA

NEARER
SPAIN

FURTHER
SPAIN

Areas under direct Roman control

Areas under Roman influence

the countries concerned, though they may not have liked the ruler that Rome supported, at least had a relatively stable government, and usually one which they knew from long experience.

One difficulty of using client kings in this way was that no king lived for ever. In the eastern part of modern Turkey, an area containing several flourishing Greek cities, the Romans used the kingdom of Pergamum as the controlling power. Although relations between the senate and the kings of Pergamum were not always smooth, the arrangement worked well from the Roman point of view, and the territory of Pergamum had been extended to cover a substantial area inland from the western coast of Asia Minor. In 133 Attalus III, the last of the Pergamene kings, died and in his will left his kingdom to the Roman people. The new province, which the Romans called Asia, was an extremely rich area, and although it immediately involved Rome in a series of bitter wars, the inheritance was accepted.

One other province on the shore of the Mediterranean was acquired by Rome in a similar way. This was the kingdom of Cyrene, which lay to the west of Egypt, left to Rome by its king, Ptolemy Apion, at his death in 96 BC. This time, however, the Romans were less eager to take over responsibility, perhaps because the north African coast did not have the obvious advantages of the wealthy cities of Asia. For whatever reason, it was more than twenty years before Cyrenaica became a Roman province, in 74 BC.

GRADUAL EXPANSION

Although there was a real reluctance to send Roman troops overseas for long periods, and thus to expand the Roman empire during this period, it would be wrong to imagine that all the provinces acquired were forced upon an unwilling Rome. In 121 BC after a series of campaigns the southern coast of France was annexed, and became known as the province of *Gallia Transalpina* (Gaul-on-the-far-side-of-the-Alps), or *Gallia Narbonensis*, after the Roman colony of Narbo, planted in the area three years later. The major reasons for this move by the Romans were almost certainly strategic. The route from Italy to the provinces in Spain led along that coastline, and at a time when land-transport was much more reliable than sea-transport, control of that route was of great importance to them. What was more, possession of the area would give Rome and Italy some protection against the danger of invasion from the great migrating tribes which were at this time beginning to appear further north.

Another similar instance was the decision in the early first century BC to turn northern Italy, from the valley of the Po north to the Alps, into the province of *Gallia Cisalpina* (Gaul-on this-side-of-the-Alps – so called because of the Gallic tribes who lived there). This was an area fought over by Roman armies for over one hundred and fifty years before being given the status of a regular province. Once again the strategic importance of maintaining a close watch over the gateway to Italy is clear. What is most surprising, with both Gallia Cisalpina and Gallia Narbonensis, is that the Romans did not decide to put their control over these areas on a regular footing long before.

THE FIRST TWO CENTURIES OF THE EMPIRE

In the crucial period when Rome progressed from being a purely Italian power to one established as mistress of the Mediterranean, it was not the aim of her policies to acquire a long list of provinces. This is shown by the way she used the client kings to rule on her behalf. The senate seemed much more interested in making Rome's presence felt and in achieving whatever ends concerned her at the time, than in directly governing large stretches of territory. Indeed when Polybius said of 167 BC that at that time almost the entire world was under Roman control, he did not mean that it was all governed as provinces. Then large parts of the Mediterranean coast still belonged to states which were in theory independent of Rome, and ranged from the native kingdoms of the north African coast, through the principalities of Asia Minor to the great Hellenistic kingdoms of Syria and Egypt in the eastern Mediterranean. But despite this, Polybius was in no doubt that, by 167, Rome was the chief world power. She did not need provinces to achieve this position and, in some cases, as we have seen with Asia and Cyrenaica, she gained the provinces by being the main power in the area, rather than needing the provinces in order to become powerful.

The provinces away from the Mediterranean

It was inevitable that as Roman power increased, more and more states should be drawn under her influence, and almost inevitable

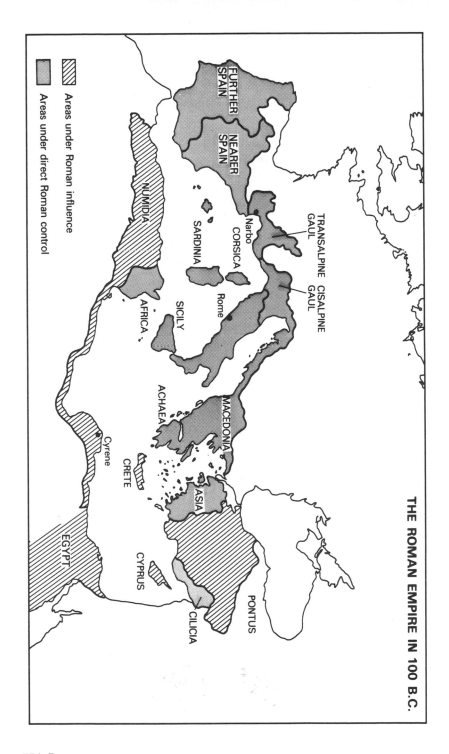

THE ROMAN EMPIRE IN 100 B.C.

Areas under Roman influence

Areas under direct Roman control

FURTHER SPAIN

NEARER SPAIN

NUMIDIA

SARDINIA

CORSICA

Narbo

TRANSALPINE GAUL

CISALPINE GAUL

AFRICA

SICILY

Rome

ACHAEA

MACEDONIA

Cyrene

CRETE

ASIA

EGYPT

CYPRUS

CILICIA

PONTUS

that in time a number of these areas would come to be directly administered by the Romans themselves. What was far from inevitable was that Rome's power should extend from the firm base it had created on the shores of the Mediterranean to inland areas both in the east and, more noticeably, to the north. The ancient civilisations of Greece, Rome and Carthage had, after all, sat 'like frogs round a pond' as Socrates said of the Greeks, with their ideas centred on the sea, whose name, Mediterranean, still declares that it lies at the middle of the world. Despite this, Rome came eventually to govern such far-off areas as northern France and Britain, and parts of the coasts of the Red Sea and (for a brief period) of the Caspian Sea. As a result, Rome became the first truly European empire, with an influence that was not confined to the enclosed circle of the Mediterranean basin. At the same time she was spreading awareness of Greek and Roman ideas and institutions to regions far away from that central sea.

A PERIOD OF EXPANSION: 79–44 BC

Rome's expansion in the last years of the Republic, from the death of the dictator Sulla in 79 BC down to the murder of Julius Caesar in 44 BC, was mainly in two areas: Asia Minor and the east coast of the Mediterranean, and Gallia Transalpina (essentially modern France). In the east, Roman involvement resulted from the Roman presence in the province of Asia, and from the ambitions of the king of one of the half-Greek half-native states that made up the remainder of Asia Minor. This was Mithridates VI, King of Pontus, on the south-east coast of the Black Sea. His desire to extend his kingdom throughout Asia Minor and even into Greece itself led to a long and hard-fought series of wars between 95 and 63 BC, when he was finally defeated by a large Roman force under Pompey.

As a result of these wars Roman influence was strengthened throughout much of the eastern Mediterranean and Asia Minor, and this can be seen in the arrangements left by Pompey after Mithridates had finally been driven into exile and to suicide in 63 BC. By then there were already three Roman provinces in the area, Asia (a province since 133); Bithynia on the Black Sea coast to the west of Pontus, which had been bequeathed to Rome by its king in 74; and Cilicia, a small enclave on the Mediterranean coast which had been annexed, probably as a base against pirates, in 100. When Pompey came to reorganise the area, Rome controlled the whole of the

1   *Mithridates VI of Pontus*

2   *A bust of Pompey (in profile and full face)*

peninsula of Asia Minor, and the eastern Mediterranean coast from modern Turkey down as far as Egypt.

Although the size of the problem facing him was larger than any in previous Roman experience, the solutions Pompey adopted were basically those we have already seen. He did create a new province of Syria, and extended Cilicia and Bithynia so that they covered much larger stretches of the Black Sea coast and the Mediterranean coast respectively. But the rest of the territory he divided between a series of client kings, dependent on Roman military and diplomatic support, who were to govern their kingdoms on a semi-independent basis.

However the first real change, away from avoiding direct provincial administration as much as possible, came with Caesar's arrangements in Gaul. When he took over the Gallic provinces after his consulship in 59 BC, they consisted of Gallia Cisalpina in northern Italy, and Gallia Transalpina, along the southern coast of France. Rome was called in to help one of the Gallic tribes which was under pressure as a result of the large-scale movements of population in the area. In the next eight years Caesar subdued the whole of Gaul, from the frontiers of the old province of Transalpina to the English Channel and from the Rhine to the Atlantic coast, and brought it under Roman rule, as well as finding time for two brief raids into Britain. In Gaul, however, the system of client kingdoms was not used. This was partly because of the threat to Italy posed by any major migrations of population from Gaul to the south, a threat of which the Romans were always acutely conscious; partly too it was because the chaotic state of relations between the different tribal groups in Gaul had given the senate cause for anxiety before. In any case, when Caesar eventually left the Gallic provinces in 49 BC to march against Rome, the whole area was under direct Roman rule, and was to remain so as long as the empire lasted.

THE INFLUENCE OF CAESAR AND POMPEY

Both Caesar and Pompey had brought great stretches of the ancient world under Roman influence of one sort or another. It had become clear, both in the long wars in the east which led to Pompey's victory over Mithridates and during Caesar's ten years in Gaul, that the growth of Roman power and Roman responsibilities gave rise to military situations in which a single commander would have large numbers of soldiers at his disposal for long periods of time.

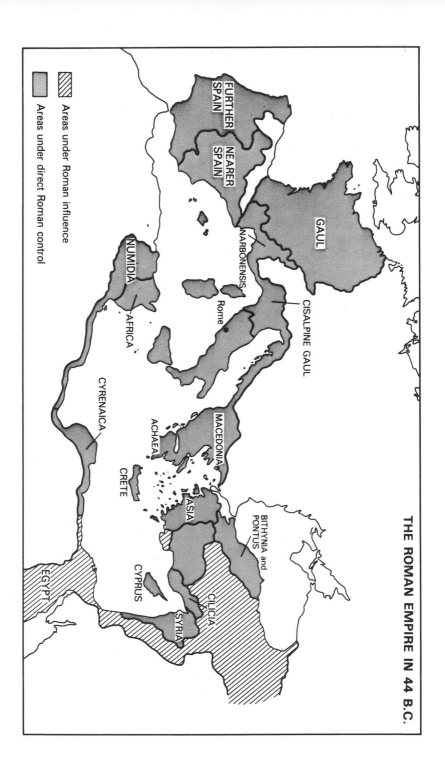

THE ROMAN EMPIRE IN 44 B.C.

Areas under direct Roman control

Areas under Roman influence

FURTHER SPAIN

NEARER SPAIN

GAUL

NARBONENSIS

CISALPINE GAUL

NUMIDIA

Rome

AFRICA

CYRENAICA

MACEDONIA

ACHAEA

CRETE

ASIA

BITHYNIA and PONTUS

CYPRUS

CILICIA

SYRIA

EGYPT

3 *Julius Caesar*

The chief danger here lay in the large size of the forces under the control of these individuals, compared with the ability of the state to protect itself from them if they chose to use such forces against the state itself. The position was made worse because the men chosen for large tasks of this kind often possessed considerable ability and great ambition. It was this imbalance and this ambition that made inevitable the great clash between Caesar and the senate, with Pompey as its general, which caused the civil war from 49 to 45 BC, and the final fall of the republic in Rome.

The early empire: Augustus and his successors

The reign of Augustus, from his defeat of Marcus Antonius (Mark Antony) in 31 BC, which left him as master of the Roman world, to his death in AD 14, marks the largest single expansion of the provinces of the Roman empire. In Spain, he supervised the conquest of the north-west corner of the peninsula, completing the process that had begun two centuries earlier when Roman forces had first landed south of the Pyrenees. Along the line of the River

Danube, he added the provinces of Moesia, Pannonia, Noricum and Raetia, stretching from the Black Sea coast in the east to modern Switzerland in the west. Another province, Illyricum in the western part of modern Yugoslavia, linked this group both with the Adriatic coast and with the already existing province of Macedonia in the south.

The situation in Asia Minor and Syria was left unchanged by Augustus; the arrangements there were basically those Pompey had instituted in 63 BC, with various changes in detail made by Antonius during his period in the east, before his defeat at Actium in 31 BC. As well as these, Augustus also added the kingdom of Egypt to the areas under Roman control, and although not a province in the same sense that the others were, it was directly governed by the Roman emperor.

AUGUSTUS AND THE GROWTH OF THE EMPIRE

This immense expansion in the number of provinces is clearly on a different scale from the gradual increase that we have seen under the republic. The reasons for this change are not obvious or straightforward. Several modern writers on Augustus have assumed that his idea was to establish an easily defensible frontier, especially along the rivers in the north, the Rhine and the Danube. It is quite likely that he did not want to have more troops in the army than he could help, particularly because it was the existence of large armies in the provinces that had made possible the rise of the great generals in the last years of the republic who, like Julius Caesar, had been able to use them to overturn the established government. As Augustus himself was now the establishment, he might reasonably have tried to prevent this happening again. Certainly some of his conquests, for example in Spain, look like an attempt to tidy up the shape of Rome's possessions, and the line of the frontier that Augustus left in the north, running down the Rhine from its mouth on the North Sea to Lake Constance on the boundary between Germany and Switzerland, and along the Danube from southern Germany to the Black Sea, was a shorter and more clearly marked one than had existed before.

We must remember however that Augustus' contemporaries did not see his additions to the empire as the result of careful calculations about lengths and defensibility of frontiers. The poets of the time make much of the glorious conquests he had achieved and of the limitless possibilities for further extension of the Roman dominions. Thus the Roman poet Horace could write, in about 13 BC:

> None shall break the emperor's edicts, not those who drink from the deep waters of the Danube, nor the Getae nor the Chinese nor the faithless Persians, nor those born beside the river Don.
>
> [Horace, *Odes* IV 15]

There is certainly exaggeration here – not even Horace can have imagined that Augustus intended to conquer China. But the main point is clear. Augustus is seen as a great conqueror who will go on from strength to strength. It may be of course that this was merely propaganda, put about by the emperor to bolster his image, but the detailed evidence of the way he treated the frontier, especially in the north (the Rhine–Danube line) suggests that his ideas were not mainly defensive.

As Romans were to find later, rivers did not make good defensive barriers to keep out attacks from the tribes living outside the empire. Though an enemy would need to cross them, rivers in the ancient world were mainly used for transport, and it was always possible for a band of barbarian troops to sail down a river until they reached an easy place to disembark. Rivers do make good boundaries between one piece of territory and another, so that no Roman and no foreigner from outside could be in any doubt about whether he was inside the frontier or not. But a river is not an easily defended obstacle, and indeed Augustus' military camps were stationed some way back from the rivers themselves. He was apparently more interested in marking out how much territory the Romans claimed to be administering directly, than in making the empire easy to defend.

For most of his reign Augustus seems to be involved in an expansionist drive to enlarge the Roman provinces. In AD 9, however, five years before his death, a Roman army was wiped out in northern Germany, and its commander P. Quinctilius Varus, committed suicide. The biographer Suetonius described Augustus' reaction:

> They say that he was so overwhelmed with grief that for months on end he did not cut his beard or his hair, and sometimes struck his head against the doors, shouting, 'Quinctilius Varus, bring back the

legions'. Every year he kept the day of the disaster as one of sadness and mourning.   [Suetonius, *Life of Augustus* 23]

The impact of this loss was not only on Augustus' state of mind, but also on his foreign policy, for from this time on he seems to have abandoned the idea of further conquest on the northern frontier, and to have established larger legionary bases at Strasbourg (Argentorate) behind the Rhine in eastern France and at Vindonissa in northern Switzerland. Though these arrangements were still not strongly defensive, there is no sign after AD 9 of any attempts at further expansion. This is summed up in the advice that Augustus gave to his successor, Tiberius, that the empire should be 'kept within its existing boundaries'.

FROM AUGUSTUS TO TRAJAN

If the reign of Augustus was an age of expansion of the Roman provinces, the rest of the first century AD was essentially one of consolidation. With one exception, the area of Roman influence remained within the bounds which Augustus had reached, though within that area the emperors continued the process we have seen under the republic of taking under their direct administration some regions which had previously been governed by client kings, dependent on Roman support. Into this category came the north African kingdom of Mauretania, Thrace on the northern side of the Bosphorus, and several of the client kingdoms of Asia Minor. In addition, part of Augustus' northern frontier was altered to make it easier to defend: an awkward corner of the River Rhine in the Black Forest area was cut off by a defensive wall, begun by the emperors Vespasian and Domitian in the 70s and 80s AD.

The one major addition was the island of Britain. The poets writing under Augustus had added this to the list of areas that the emperor would conquer in due course, but in fact he seems to have shown little interest in it. It was left to the emperor Claudius, in AD 42, to launch the invasion, largely in an attempt to demonstrate that, although he seemed the least warlike of the early emperors, he too could be a conqueror in the tradition of Julius Caesar and of Augustus. There were several set-backs and advances in the conquest of the island, but by the time that the emperor Hadrian (AD 117–138) ordered the building of the frontier wall which now bears his name, most of Britain south of that line was under Roman control.

At the very end of the first century AD, there appeared another emperor who seemed intent on restarting the policy of conquest that Augustus had finally abandoned. This was Trajan (AD 98–117). The last Roman to extend significantly the boundaries of the empire, he fought with success both north of the Danube and east of the Euphrates, so that, even though his successor Hadrian had to withdraw from some of the larger areas he had captured, nevertheless Arabia and Dacia were added to the list of provinces. In the latter, though the Romans were forced to abandon it a century and a half later, they left such a mark that the country is still known as the land of the Romans, or Roumania.

Conclusion

The shape of Rome's empire around the Mediterranean sea, northwards into Europe and eastwards into the Middle East was first laid out by the generals of the republic, culminating in the last and most spectacular of them, Caesar and Pompey. That shape, filled out by the great conquests of Augustus and consolidated by his successors, was to remain essentially unchanged for over four hundred years – a remarkable achievement, unequalled in the western world. As we shall see, it was precisely in the great periods of expansion during the republic and early empire that the Romans developed their ideas and methods of provincial administration, and those ideas and methods, though elaborated by later generations, remained basically the same through much of the later empire. What we must now look at is how Rome set about controlling the world that she had won.

2

The governor in his province: the republican period

FROM the late third century BC onwards, the Romans were faced with the problem of controlling and administering the provinces that they had acquired. By the period of the late republic (the first century BC) they had established a number of methods and institutions for this purpose. The best way to understand these developments is to see how the governors of the late republic worked in practice, and we are especially fortunate in this. Cicero, the most prolific writer to survive from that time, was himself a provincial governor late in his career, and even before that had been much involved with other governors. Thus the two men whose governorships we know most about are probably Cicero himself, who was in charge in Cilicia between 51 and 50 BC; and Gaius Verres, who was governor in Sicily between 73 and 70 BC, and who, as a result of his misgovernment, was successfully prosecuted by Cicero on his return to Rome.

CICERO AND VERRES: THE SOURCES

In what follows I have concentrated particularly on the careers of these two men, but before discovering what the sources tell us about their governorships, it is important to remember what the sources themselves are like. We hear of Cicero's period in Cilicia from the letters he himself wrote to his friends in Rome while he was in the province, especially to the rich banker T. Pomponius Atticus, with whom he kept up a correspondence for over twenty years of his life as a politician.[1] Consequently, it is Cicero's views on his governorship that we have, and though he is sometimes

[1] See also David Taylor: *Cicero and Rome*, in this series, esp. pp. 11–12.

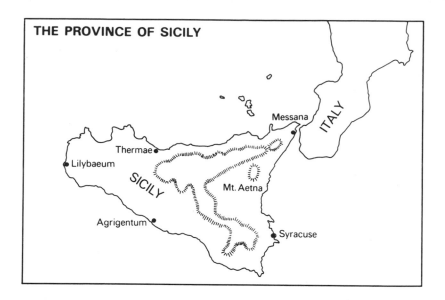

THE PROVINCE OF SICILY

Messana

ITALY

Thermae

Lilybaeum

SICILY

Mt. Aetna

Agrigentum

Syracuse

amazingly open and frank about his dealings, it is inevitable that the impression he gives is a favourable one. Verres' time in Sicily on the other hand is known purely from the speeches that Cicero wrote in 70 BC accusing him of fraud, maladministration and quite amazing cruelty while he was there. It is only Cicero's version of these events that has survived. We never hear what Verres himself might have had to say, and neither in fact did the Roman jury that condemned him. After hearing Cicero's first brief but damning speech, Verres decided he stood no chance of acquittal, and rapidly withdrew from Rome altogether, leaving Cicero to publish the longer and more detailed speeches which he had written to use in the trial, but which in the event he had no opportunity to deliver in court. As a result, the picture we have of Cicero's governorship is largely favourable, while that of Verres' is totally hostile.

The governor and his staff

When the senate had first needed to find governors for its overseas provinces, it had turned understandably to those who already had power (*imperium*) granted to them by the state. These were the city magistrates at Rome – the two consuls, who were the chief executive officers of the state, and the more junior praetors. All these officers were elected by the people of Rome to serve for one year at a time and, before they could be elected, they had to have reached a certain age. They also had to hold the magistracies in a fixed order. Thus they could not hold the quaestorship, the most junior post on the ladder of offices (called the *cursus honorum*) until they were thirty; they could not be made a praetor until they were forty, and had already held the quaestorship; and they could not become consul until the age of forty-three, and after they had held the praetorship.

THE APPOINTMENT OF THE GOVERNOR

This system of annual magistracies was designed to suit a city-state like Rome itself; it was not well adapted for the purposes of governing a province. The difficulty of travelling long distances to reach the area must have made the prospect of staying there for just twelve months seem ridiculous. More importantly, many of the provinces were crucial military areas, and in these cases a commander who was there for just one year would often only have begun to understand the countryside and the nature of his enemy when he would be forced to return to Rome. As a result, the Romans decided on a modification of the system: they extended the *imperium* of the city-magistrates (the technical term for this was *prorogatio*), who were said, after their term of office, to be acting in place of or on behalf of a consul or praetor (*pro consule* or *pro praetore*). It is worth emphasising that the words used for these men, proconsul or propraetor, do not mean that they were ex-consuls or ex-praetors. In the early days proconsuls were appointed, for example in the Spanish provinces, who had held neither of these magistracies, and later it was quite usual for an ex-praetor to be the governor there *pro consule*.

Usually, though, these pro-magistrates were men who were appointed because they had been either consul or praetor, and for most of the republican period their term as a provincial governor carried on from their period as an ordinary magistrate, and lasted two or three years. In order to avoid the charge of favouritism, the senate could not choose which province a particular governor went to. Its job was to draw up a list of provinces requiring governors, and the praetors, and usually the consuls too, were assigned to their province by the use of the lot. In the case of the

29

more important provinces that were assigned to the consuls, a law passed by the radical tribune Gaius Gracchus in 123 or 122 BC went so far as to insist that the provinces should be chosen even before the consuls were elected, usually six months before they entered office.

THE GOVERNOR'S QUAESTOR

In practice, then, the republican provincial governors were men who had been elected to a magistracy by the Roman people. As such they were not chosen especially for the tasks that they would have to perform overseas, and this placed added importance on the staff that they took with them to their provinces. The choice of one of the most important of these, the quaestor, was not left to the governor. He was a junior magistrate, elected by the people and assigned to a particular province by lot, just like the governor' himself. The quaestor was in charge of the finances of the province, and the governor, although he had not chosen him, often assigned extra duties to him connected with its administration. Thus Cicero left his quaestor in charge, when he left his province in 50 BC, eager to return to Rome – even though, as Cicero admitted to Atticus in a letter, he was 'a mere boy and probably stupid, frivolous and incapable of self-restraint' [*Letters to Atticus* VI 6.3].

THE LEGATI

In the case of other members of his staff, however, the governor did have some choice. The most important of these staff-officers were his immediate subordinates, the *legati*, who would have to carry out much of the work that the governor himself did not have time for. These men were, properly speaking, appointed by the senate, but usually the governor himself recommended those he would like to have with him. Cicero took four such assistants, two of whom we know to have had experience in provincial administration before: one, Gaius Pomptinus, had been governor in Transalpine Gaul, where he had had considerable military success; another, Cicero's brother Quintus, had administered the rich and peaceful province of Asia for three years. In addition to these, the governor himself had the power to appoint minor military commanders, known generally as *praefecti*.

As well as the expertise of his chosen *legati*, there was another source of assistance open to the governor. This was the body of *apparitores*, who might be described as professional civil servants of a minor kind. These men, clerks, messengers, heralds and so forth, were organised by the state into professional bodies and drew a regular salary. Any city magistrate or provincial governor would draw his staff from these bodies, probably again by lot, before taking up office. In the case of the provinces, these minor civil servants are unlikely to have known much about the particular region they were going to, as they were drawn from Rome, not the province itself, but they would have a considerable knowledge of administration in general.

Finally there was one other group of men who accompanied the governor to his province: these were the *comites*, usually young men invited to go abroad in order to gain experience, and usually also personal friends and relations of the governor. Thus Cicero took with him his own son and nephew, and also a young relative of his friend and correspondent Atticus. These men too could be delegated by the governor to do various jobs in the province.

The staff a governor took with him was not large, but it did contain certain men who knew something about provincial administration, and its effect both for good and bad could be considerable. In his attack on Verres, Cicero detailed some of the crimes committed by the associates and by the *apparitores* (especially the *scriba*, or chief clerk), and summed up the position by saying that the band of attendants 'did more damage to Sicily than would have been done by a hundred bands of runaway slaves' [Cicero, *Second Verrines* IV 27].

The governor's tasks

The provincial governor had reached his position of authority because he had been able to attract the votes of the people of Rome. Yet once he was in his province, his power was to all intents and purposes absolute. In particular, whatever the reasons had been for his election at Rome, he was commander-in-chief of the Roman forces within his province. Though he would certainly have had some military experience early in his career, the Roman magistrate was certainly not a professional soldier, and might well have spent most of his life in the civilian world of politics at Rome.

This, then, is how Cicero came to be in charge of the two legions of Roman soldiers based in Cilicia in 51 BC. He was aged 55; his last military experience had been, so far as we know, as a young man of 18. If his Cilician legions had been at full strength (which we know they were not) he would have had about 12,000 Roman soldiers under his direct control and a mountainous and difficult area in which to keep the peace and to repel any invaders from outside.

In fact, in the early stages of his governorship, it looked as though Cilicia might face a foreign invasion, for the forces of the Parthian empire, Rome's great rival in the Middle East, were reported to have invaded Syria, the province immediately to the east of Cilicia. Cicero, as he later reported back to the senate, led out his troops to secure the somewhat doubtful loyalty of the client kingdoms on his borders, and then moved towards the Syrian frontier. At this point the Parthians, who had been checked by forces under a legate of the proconsul of Syria, withdrew, so that Cicero's military prowess was not put to the test.

However he did have other, if less spectacular, involvements in military affairs. Cilicia, like many provinces of the empire, was plagued by organised bands of brigands in the mountainous regions, against whom Cicero led a successful expedition, once the Parthian menace had vanished. He captured a bandit stronghold at Pindenessus, and had the satisfaction of being hailed as *imperator* by his soldiers, which was their way of recognising a victory. He even hoped, vainly as it turned out, that he might be awarded the supreme distinction of a triumph by the senate on his return to Rome.

This type of military activity might occur in almost any of the provinces. Even in Sicily, one of the most peaceful provinces in the last decades of the republic, the military and naval forces had to be kept up to scratch, particularly because of the threat from pirates. Cicero describes how, because of Verres' negligence, the position in Sicily became so bad that pirates could actually sail into the Great Harbour at Syracuse, which, he claims, had previously been thought to be impregnable:

> What a miserable, what a bitter spectacle! The glory of Rome and the reputation of the Roman people were made a laughing-stock in front of a vast number of people by a pirate galley! In the very harbour of Syracuse a pirate ship celebrated a triumph over the fleet of the Roman people, while its oars splashed water into the eyes of that shiftless and worthless governor!
>
> [Cicero, *Second Verrines* V 100]

The governor was of course responsible for the upkeep of his military forces, not just for leading them in battle. Cicero claims that during Verres' time in Sicily, the Roman forces had to scrounge the roots of wild palm trees to eat, while the pirates lived off the corn for which the island was famous. He was also, during his own time in Cilicia, bitterly critical of the way in which his predecessor had allowed the forces to run down. In fact, when he took over the province, Cicero had to write to the previous governor complaining that three cohorts at full strength (about 1,800 men) were missing, and that he didn't know where they were.

It is worth noticing that neither Cicero nor Verres were in particularly warlike areas. Their provinces could not compare in this respect with, say, Caesar's province of Transalpine Gaul, nor with the Spanish provinces, which saw almost continuous fighting for two hundred years. But despite the generally peaceful nature of Sicily and even of Cilicia, it is clear that even there the Roman governor was above all else the representative of Rome's military might in the area and commander-in-chief of the Roman forces on the spot.

THE LAW COURTS

The other task that took up much of a governor's time was just as technical a matter as leading the army: he was responsible for deciding a large number of the major law cases in his province. Both Cicero and Verres spent a lot of time in the courts – roughly speaking five months of the twelve Cicero spent in Cilicia were chiefly occupied with military matters, and seven with civilian affairs, especially justice and administration. Even Caesar at the end of his annual campaigns in Transalpine Gaul crossed the Alps to preside at the courts in Cisalpine Gaul.

Once again, as with the military duties, it might well happen that a particular governor was not expert in legal matters. Many Roman politicians had a great deal to do with the courts in Rome, as Cicero did for example, and often when they held the praetorship in the city, they presided over one of the courts. On the other hand, just as with military affairs, a particular governor might have little technical expertise, and need to depend on members of his staff, who sat with him in court to give advice.

LEX PROVINCIAE

There was another difficulty as well. The law which the governor administered was similar to, but not exactly the same as the law he might have come across in Rome. The outline was laid down in a special law for the province, the *lex provinciae*, usually drawn up by a commission of ten senators at the time the province was taken under direct Roman control. The main difference was that whereas in Rome itself Roman law applied to all citizens, and to non-citizens who were involved with citizens in a law suit, in the provinces much of the ordinary business of the courts came under the jurisdiction of the cities in the provinces themselves and was administered by the magistrates of those cities. The governor was, usually, directly responsible for cases where there was a dispute between citizens from two different provincial cities, or in which a Roman citizen was involved. Even in such cases, there were often local regulations which laid down where the case should be heard (an important matter in the ancient world, where travel was slow and expensive) and also the details of the procedure to be followed.

THE GOVERNOR'S EDICT

The other major source of law from the Roman side came from the governor himself. On taking up the post in his province, the governor issued an edict, stating the grounds on which he was prepared to hear cases, just as the praetors in charge of the courts in Rome had to do. A certain amount of what was contained in the edict was probably handed on from one governor to the next, but each had a fairly free hand in what he added or subtracted. Thus Cicero, drafting his edict before he left Rome, included a large traditional section, no doubt containing the ordinary law for the province, and also stated that he would follow the edicts of the praetors in the city of Rome. But he was able for his own part to add a section on the finances of the cities under his control, and on inheritance and private law. He had to be particularly careful how these parts were worded, as he could be held to them by those coming to court, and on the interpretation of them would depend much of the success or failure of the changes he was trying to introduce.

JURISDICTION WITHIN THE PROVINCE

Despite all these complications, the governor had a great deal of power in his own courts. With certain exceptions, he could punish anyone in his province with flogging or death, as well as with large-scale confiscation of property. The exceptions were firstly Roman citizens who, unless they were in the army, had the right of appeal to the Roman people for a trial before an assembly (the *iudicium populi*), if they were condemned to either flogging or death by a provincial governor. Also certain cities in the provinces had specific treaties with Rome, which protected their citizens, so that the governor's jurisdiction over men from these allied communities (the *civitates foederatae*) was restricted. Another category which had some legal privileges were the 'free' cities (*civitates liberae*), and here too the governor had to be careful about interfering with local law courts. The distribution of these two types throughout the provinces was uneven (thus all the cities in Greece were 'free' while in Sicily there were just five 'free' and two 'allied') but the majority had no special privileges of this sort, and could come under the direct weight of the governor's administration of justice.

If the powers of the governor were large in theory, in practice they tended to be larger still. In Rome a praetor in his court was under the eyes of the whole city, and this inevitably imposed a check on the extent of his activities, whereas in the provinces the governor was much more nearly a free agent, despite the legal limits on his jurisdiction. As Cicero wrote to his brother Quintus, commending his leniency while he was governor in Asia:

> How delightful it is to see gentleness in a praetor in Asia, in a province in which such a vast number of citizens and of allies, so many towns and cities depend upon the whim of one man, but where there is no legal sanction, no procedure for complaints, no public assembly! [Cicero, *Letters to his brother Quintus* I 1.22]

Needless to say under such circumstances, not all provincial governors showed the same clemency that Cicero saw in his brother's administration of the law. A man who set out to misuse the powers he had could not only exert his will with very little hindrance, but could also make himself very rich in the process. As Cicero again points out in his accusation of Verres:

> No one can doubt that everyone's entire wealth is placed in the power of those who arrange the courts and who judge in them, for none of you, members of the jury, could keep his house, his farm or his ancestral property if, whenever anyone claimed them from you, a corrupt praetor, against whom no sanction was possible, appointed a judge of his choice, a worthless judge, who would judge just as the praetor instructed.   [Cicero, *Second Verrines* II 30]

4   *A bust of Cicero*

And according to Cicero, this is just what Verres did, encouraging complaints against anyone who had received a large inheritance, so that he and the complainant could split the proceeds.

The governor was the main source of justice in his province, once a case had been taken beyond the level of the local courts administered by the provincials themselves. This is not really surprising, for he, more than anyone else, had the power to enforce his decisions through his control of the military forces; but it added still further to the great power the governor had within his province, both for good and for ill.

FINANCIAL RESPONSIBILITIES

The financial responsibilities of the governor were complicated by the fact that, even more than is true of the regulations concerning jurisdiction, the system of taxation varied considerably from one province to another. Most provinces paid a tax or *stipendium*, which was paid at a fixed amount each year, usually in money, but in some places in goods. The details of its organisation varied from place to place, because the Romans had usually adapted the system of taxation they found in the area when they moved into it. In Sicily, Sardinia and Asia, however, the tax was not the fixed *stipendium* but a payment of a tithe (*decuma*), that is one-tenth part of the crops harvested. In either case, the governor's responsibility might be restricted by the status of some of the cities in his province, just as we have seen with his jurisdiction. 'Allied' cities were exempt from these taxes, and so were a small number of the 'free' cities, which had been given the extra privilege of immunity from taxation. In addition to these main taxes, there were also other less important levies, especially customs duties (*portoria*) collected on goods passing through the ports and across the frontiers of the provinces.

COLLECTION OF TAXES

The financial duties of a governor in his province would depend on the particular sort of taxes collected there. There is no doubt that he was in a sense responsible for the whole process, if only because he was the chief source of law, and the taxes were regulated by law. The *stipendium*, which was a fairly simple tax to collect, was probably handled directly by the quaestor, as the governor's financial officer, and his staff. The tithes, however, and the other minor forms of taxation, which varied in the amount of money they produced, depending on the size of the harvest or the amount of trade going through the ports of the province, were not collected by the governor's staff at all, but by the representatives of private companies, who had bought the right to collect the tax from the state. In Sicily, which was a special case, individuals or groups of individuals, many of them from the province itself, negotiated this purchase with the governor in Syracuse. In all the other cases we know of, the rights were sold by auction in Rome by the censors (the magistrates responsible, among other things, for allotting the contracts for public building work), and these contracts ran for a period of five years.

PUBLICANI

The use of these companies, owned by private individuals, known as *publicani*, seems strange to us, used as we are to taxation being very much in the hands of the state and of its civil service. For the Romans it seemed just as natural to have a private company collecting taxes as doing anything else for the state. The arrangements for tax-collecting were run on the same lines as those for providing equipment for the army or for erecting public buildings and aqueducts, and probably the same companies of financiers would bid for both sorts of contract.

What is more, the system had certain clear advantages for the Romans. We have seen that the governor's staff was not large, and to have taken on all the work involved in taxation as well would have forced the republic to employ a large number of additional men, skilled in financial matters. They avoided this by using the *publicani* to do the job for them. There was one other advantage that was perhaps even more important. The *stipendium*, which the governor's staff collected themselves, was a fixed tax, and would, if properly collected, produce a known amount of money and goods; the taxes collected by the *publicani* were bound to give a variable revenue. By fixing a price for the *publicani* to pay the state for a period of five years, the censors would know how much money they would get in that period. It was the *publicani* who had to take account of the variations in making their offer for the contract, and who would do well in good years and badly in poor ones.

The disadvantages of the system affected not so much the Romans as the provincials themselves. The agents of the *publicani* in the provinces were obviously out to make a profit for their financial backers in Rome and for themselves, so that they were likely to be unscrupulous in exacting money from the provincials. The historian Livy, writing after the end of the republic about an earlier decision by the senate not to use *publicani* on one occasion, remarked that

> wherever there is a *publicanus*, either the public law is disregarded, or the liberty of the allies is reduced to nothing.   [Livy XLV 18.4]

Similarly Cicero says of the provincials in Sicily, where the work usually done by Roman *publicani* was auctioned locally, that 'they alone do not regard a *publicanus* or a business man with hatred.' [Cicero, *Second Verines* II 7]

TRANSFER OF MONEY IN THE ANCIENT WORLD

There was one other way in which the publican companies were especially useful and therefore especially important to the state and the governors. By far the greatest part of the income of the Roman state came from the provinces, but it was also in the provinces that most of it was spent. In fact Cicero says in a speech delivered in 66 BC that of all the provinces that Rome ruled, only Asia returned a substantial profit. While this may be an exaggeration, it is certain that the bulk of Rome's expenditure would be on the army in the provinces, and in particular on feeding it and paying its wages.

For this reason it would have been absurd to move the money paid in taxation back to Rome from the provinces, only to return it there. It is worth remembering that transferring money in the ancient world was a laborious business, involving ship-loads and wagon-loads of silver coin and bullion, which it was hard and expensive work to transport. What is more, there was always a very real risk that the cash would be seized in transit by pirates or brigands. Therefore the representatives of the *publicani*, who were holding considerable amounts of cash collected as taxation, were very useful. Verres, for example, drew money from the companies operating in Sicily to purchase corn for his own and his staff's use.

THE GOVERNOR'S ALLOWANCE

This money which Verres received from the tax-company in Sicily formed part of the allowance (*vasarium*) granted to a provincial governor by the senate. In the strict sense of the word, the governors did not receive payment for their services, which were looked on as duties which they owed to the state. But they did have very considerable allowance made for expenses. In addition to money, either taken with them from Rome or drawn from the publican companies in the provinces, they had the right to a certain amount of corn which was requisitioned from the provincials for the upkeep of themselves and their staff. In addition to this, the senate fixed the price at which they could buy extra corn, and the farmers in the province had to provide it at that price.

HONEST AND DISHONEST GOVERNORS

The allowance made by the senate seems to have been very generous, and, properly speaking, the governor should only have taken for himself what he actually spent. As the things he was allowed to spend it on were strictly controlled by law, at least at the end of the republic, it was possible for an honest governor to return a substantial amount of his allowance to the state. At the end of his year in Cilicia, Cicero deposited 2,200,000 sesterces which he had been able to save through careful management. This was a very large sum – twice as much as was needed in property to qualify to be a senator in the early empire. The difficulty was that a dishonest governor could easily find ways to pocket this money himself. There were other ways too in which, by using the senate's own regulations, a governor could make a profit for himself out of the unfortunate provincials. For instance Cicero accuses Verres of ordering farmers in Sicily not merely to sell him corn, but to transport it at their own expense to the other end of the island, and to deliver it on the same day that he issued the order. As this was impossible, he 'allowed' them to pay him for the corn instead, at a price that he fixed himself! Verres is also accused of other swindles over corn that he was supposed to purchase to send to Rome. When the corn was delivered, he refused it on the grounds that the quality was below standard, exacted a cash payment instead, and sent to Rome in its place corn from his own surplus stocks, for which he charged the state an extremely high price.

Once again, despite the legal restrictions placed upon the governor, and the fact that much of the taxation was taken out of his hands, the position of supreme authority which he had in his province meant that in practice he could get away with all sorts of improper deals. Most of these did not damage the Roman state directly, but the provincials were likely to suffer greatly at the hands of an unscrupulous man.

Pressures on the provincial governor

It was inevitable that, because a governor was so powerful in his province, all sorts of people should attempt to influence him to use that power in their favour. To a large extent, the way in which he handled these pressures determined the way in which his governorship would go.

THE PROVINCIALS

First of all there were those among the provincials who wanted the backing of the governor for their own schemes, whether legal or not. Verres, so Cicero said, confiscated inheritances from rich Sicilians, following complaints from other Sicilians who were associates of Verres himself. In a similar fashion Cicero alleges that the collectors of the Sicilian corn-tithe, many of whom were Sicilians, successfully bribed Verres to sell the rights to the tithe to them – and to ignore their methods of collecting it – by providing him with money and women.

THE PUBLICANI

But much heavier pressure could be put on the governor by Romans. As we have seen, the *publicani* were of great importance to the governor, and Cicero for example took great care, when drafting his edict, not to offend them. Similarly he was delighted when the cities of Cilicia were able to pay their taxes in full to the tax-companies because the careful and humanitarian measures that he had taken had restored their finances. He says happily to Atticus that 'this has made me the especial favourite of the *publicani*' [Cicero, *Letters to Atticus* VI 2.5].

PRESSURE FROM ROME

Other problems arose from individual members of the senate in Rome. Cicero got into trouble with his predecessor in Cilicia, the noble Appius Claudius Pulcher, for suggesting to the Cilicians that they should not spend above the legal limit in sending embassies to the senate praising Appius' governorship. Although, privately to Atticus, Cicero had described some of Appius' actions in his province as 'the monstrous deeds not of a man but of a wild beast', he also wrote long conciliatory letters to Appius saying that he was sure a man of his humanity and sense of duty would not want the Cilicians to go outside the law!

EMBARRASSING REQUESTS

Much more serious was a request from Brutus, who later, as the murderer of Julius Caesar, was to gain fame as the leader of the die-hard republican faction, that Cicero should assist his agent in Cyprus, which was part of the province of Cilicia, to collect a loan that he had made to a town council there at an astonishingly high, and illegal, rate of interest. Cicero had fixed the rate in his edict at 12 per cent, and Brutus was wanting him to lend military forces to extract a rate of 48 per cent from the unfortunate town-councillors. Cicero was badly shaken by the business, and though he resolutely refused to take the action Brutus wanted, he avoided settling the matter, and left any final decision to his successor.

Other requests came from magistrates in the city. Caelius, a friend of Cicero's, who kept him informed by letter of what was happening in Rome while Cicero was in Cilicia, was elected aedile for 50 BC and had to provide games for the entertainment of the Roman people. As a result, he sent a continual stream of letters to the province, asking for panthers to be sent for his wild-beast show, and, more worryingly for Cicero, for a special tax to be levied (the *vectigal aedilicium*) to support the expense of putting on his games. Here Cicero was more certain about what to do, and though he tried to make a joke of his refusal to send the panthers, he replied with a downright 'no' to the suggestion of the extra tax. But clearly, from the tone of his letters, Caelius had fully expected that the governor would be prepared to make the province pay for the cost of his aedileship.

The problem for a governor in dealing with requests from *publicani*, as from senators, was that these men were powerful and important in the capital. To Cicero, for example, his time in Cilicia was simply a short break from his political career in Rome. And no politician could afford to make enemies that would cause trouble once he was back in the senate. Altogether, the combination of

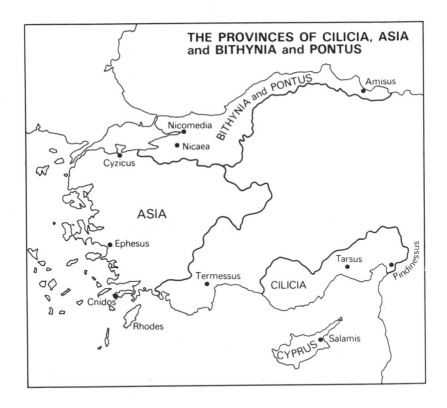

THE PROVINCES OF CILICIA, ASIA
and BITHYNIA and PONTUS

the nearly absolute powers he was granted and the pressures that could be put upon him made it extremely difficult for a governor to remain honest. When Cicero wanted to explain the basic wickedness of Verres' character, he put it like this:

> He was not corrupted by the province, as some are; he was just the same when he was in Rome. [Cicero, *Second Verrines* II 39]

The point was that even a man who was honest in Rome might be expected to yield to the pressures put on a provincial governor. Verres, on the other hand, was already corrupt before he even arrived in Sicily!

Controls on the governor

When the powers of any officer of the state are as large as were those of a provincial governor under the Roman republic, it is natural to ask what checks and controls on him were built into the state's constitutional machinery.

THE SENATE

The first place we might expect to look for a control on the governor is the senate, the body which had the largest part in running the day-to-day affairs of state. Indeed the senate did try to keep an eye on the governor's activities, and expected reports from time to time on what was happening in his province. They could even send instructions to a governor, though in practice this was a fairly rare event. What the senate, understandably enough, seems to have been most concerned about was the military activity of the governor, and the dictator Sulla laid down a detailed law in the late 80s BC, strictly limiting what a governor could and could not do. For instance, he would be guilty of treason if he declared war without the senate's permission, or led his army out of his province. The difficulty with these provisions, and with the whole idea of the senate controlling the military activities of the governor, was that the governor, because of the *imperium* that the senate had arranged for him, was in direct control of his army, and the slow communications in the ancient world over the long distances which divided the empire made him virtually independent of any authority in Rome, once he was in his province.

THE LAW COURTS IN ROME

The other method of checking the actions of the governor was by private prosecution once his governorship was over, usually to regain possession of goods and money illegally seized. The fact that the governor had to be prosecuted by a private individual, not by the state, was quite usual for the Romans, though it seems odd to us. Even a prosecution for treason under Sulla's law mentioned above was a private prosecution; there was no magistrate whose task it was to start legal proceedings against men suspected of breaking the law. At least from the time of Gaius Gracchus, who was tribune of the plebs in 123 and 122 BC, the law on recovering property (*lex de rebus repetundis*) was the main means that the provincials had of attacking a bad governor after his term of office.

The law after Gaius Gracchus certainly made an attempt to make access to the courts possible for provincials. The provincials themselves could start proceedings, and provision was made in the law for a Roman citizen to be assigned to the complaining party by the praetor in charge of the court; special facilities were granted to this prosecutor to do research in the province. Moreover, on a less formal level, provincial communities could often look for help to one or another of the great families of Rome, who were connected to them as patrons, often through an ancestor who had been important in the history of the province and its links with Rome. If the governor was found guilty, not only did he have to restore twice the value of what he had taken, but the disgrace did great damage to his future career in Rome.

DIFFICULTIES IN PROSECUTING A GOVERNOR

Nevertheless as a method of deterring governors from exploiting the provinces, this legal procedure had many weaknesses. Firstly, it was impossible to stop a governor while he was actually committing his misdeeds. The provincials could merely threaten to launch a prosecution later. Secondly, the distances and the length of time involved meant that it was an expensive business to mount a case against an ex-governor in Rome if you were a provincial landowner from, say, Spain or Syria. Again, there was inevitably a feeling among the Roman jurymen of sympathy for the governor rather than for the provincials. This is likely to have been stronger at some periods than others, for the question of who should serve on these juries became a crucial political issue in Rome, so that at different times there would for example be some senators on the jury, sometimes none, and sometimes no one but senators. This could be important, for, as Cicero shows in his speeches against Verres, the senatorial juries were suspected of favouring the governors, who were, after all, senators like themselves.

But there was one crucial disadvantage that the provincials had in undertaking a prosecution *de rebus repetundis*. It was always possible for a guilty governor to withdraw from Rome to the sanctuary of a town in the provinces. Thus Verres himself slipped off to Marseilles to live off the proceeds of his time in Sicily. In 43 BC, twenty-seven years after his condemnation, he still had enough left to attract the envy of Marcus Antonius, and in the dreadful slaughter that Antonius and the young Octavian (later known as the emperor Augustus) indulged in when first they seized power in Rome, he was killed for the sake of his property. Ironically, another victim of Antonius at this time was Cicero, whose eloquence had not only led to the condemnation of Verres, but had enraged the now all-powerful Antonius.

THE POWER OF A GOVERNOR IN HIS PROVINCE

So, as we have seen, the governor within his province was almost literally a law unto himself. He had in practice complete control over the administration of justice and much of the taxation process, and the military power to back up his decisions. To see why this was so, we must stand back a little from the details of the governor's activities, and look at the way in which the Romans, and in particular the senators, regarded the provinces which they controlled.

3

The Roman view of the provinces

To see how the provincial governor in the time of the Roman republic came to have such sweeping powers, we must look at the way in which the Romans thought of the provinces, and what sort of task they were giving a governor when first they sent him out to his province.

Province and *provincia*

The English word 'province' is so clearly derived from the Latin *provincia* that it is inevitable that we should translate the one by the other. The difficulty is that, at least during the republic, many of the associations that the word 'province' has for us were not necessarily part of the Roman idea of a *provincia*.

THE MEANING OF PROVINCIA

To us a province is a geographical area, organised for administrative purposes, and so we expect to find within a province the administrative machinery to carry on the government of that area. As we have already seen, this is true of many of the Roman provinces in the late republic; but it is important to realise that this was not the basic meaning of the word *provincia*. A *provincia* was to the Romans a field of responsibility, and usually of military responsibility. Thus *provinciae* are not geographical areas at all. During the Second Punic War (218–202 BC) for example, one of the *provinciae* of the consuls was regularly 'the war against Hannibal' without any geographical specifications. Similarly, in the field of jurisdiction, the responsibility of the city praetor (*praetor urbanus*) who was in charge of certain categories of legal cases, was described as a *provincia*; and when the senate wanted to reduce the power of Julius Caesar during and after his controversial consulship in 59 BC,

47

they assigned to him charge of the woods and footpaths of Italy, which one biographer described as 'the least important *provinciae*'.

Of course for most purposes, and in most cases, the *provincia* of a particular area – the region within which a magistrate could exercise his military authority (*imperium*) – became a province as we understand it. But the origins of the word affected the way it was used, especially in two ways which help to explain the Roman attitude to the provinces. In the first place when the senate decreed that a particular area was to be a *provincia* of a particular magistrate in the following year, it was not making a territorial claim on that area in quite the same way in which, say, the British government would be if it declared Iceland to be a colony. Thus Macedonia was assigned as a *provincia* at least as early as 213 BC, but it remained a kingdom until 167 BC and was not a province, in one sense, until 146 BC.

THE MILITARY PROVINCIA

The second point to bear in mind is that the *provincia* was from the start a military idea. The boundaries of the province, when these were fixed, were the boundaries of the governor's military power, and even in more peaceful times, his military functions were always the essential basis of his activities as governor. Thus his judicial activities, as arbitrator between Roman citizens and provincials, and between provincials themselves, especially when they were from different communities within the province, seem to have originated from Roman military power. If Rome had simply been keen on spreading the system of Roman law throughout the empire, then we would have seen a much more thorough imposition of that law at all levels. Instead the governor gave a final decision in cases where local laws did not apply, or where an appeal was made following a dispute. The reason, in practical terms, is obvious. As the commander of the military forces in the area, he had the power to enforce the decisions he reached.

Similarly the governor's overall responsibility for taxation within his province was connected with his role as commander-in-chief in the area. Originally the taxation was levied in order to pay the troops stationed there and, even in the late republic, this was the justification put forward by Roman writers. Cicero, writing to his brother Quintus, who was the governor of the peaceful and rich province of Asia, explained its taxes in these terms:

Let Asia remember that she would not enjoy this escape from the disaster of external warfare and internal strife, if she were not held by Roman power. As it would be impossible to maintain that power without the taxes, she should be happy to buy everlasting peace and freedom from worry in exchange for some part of her income.   [Cicero, *Letters to his brother Quintus* I 1.34]

In this way the functions of the provincial governor are connected to the central idea of military command; and the fact that the military command was central in turn explains why he had such far-reaching and largely uncontrolled powers. For obvious reasons it was not desirable that the decisions of a military commander should be open to question while he was still in command.

Civil administration: the local communities

In view of the strongly military bias of a governor's task, it is not surprising that he did not undertake many of the functions that would seem to us to belong naturally to the governor of an overseas possession. One obvious example which has been discussed already is that of the *publicani* who were used to collect some at least of the taxes in the provinces. Another and still larger part of the day-to-day administration was in the hands of the local communities.

Rome itself was a city-state, and consequently Roman governors found their provinces easier to manage when they were divided into units of territory based on various cities. Throughout most of the Mediterranean region such cities existed already, especially in those parts of the eastern Mediterranean and of Sicily which had been strongly influenced by Greek civilisation. Where they did not exist, as in most of Transalpine Gaul and of Spain, there was direct encouragement from the state to establish them – a process which became more marked during the period of the empire.

THE STATUS OF THE PROVINCIAL CITIES

The cities in the provinces were divided into different categories, originally because the senate favoured some, which had been notably pro-Roman, more than others. The distinctions were basically between those which were and those which were not liable to pay taxes to the state, and also between those whose right to use their own forms of law and government were specifically

guaranteed by the Roman state. Some especially favoured towns had a treaty with Rome, and were known, as mentioned in chapter 2, as *civitates foederatae* ('allied' cities). These were usually exempt from taxes, and their constitutions were not to be tampered with. For example, an inscription details the treaty with the people of Termessus, a town in Pisidia in Asia Minor (see map p. 43), stating that the citizens of the town and their descendants

> shall be free friends and allies of the Roman people and shall use their own laws; and it shall be legal for the citizens of Termessus in Pisidia to use their own laws in the manner sanctioned by this law.
> [*lex Antonia de Termessibus*, lines 5-10]

Less privileged than these were the 'free' cities, most of which did have to pay taxes, but which had the constitutional guarantees. The majority of provincial towns came into a third category of tributary cities (*civitates stipendariae*), which enjoyed neither exemption nor guarantee.

Despite these differences, all these grades of city had their own forms of local government, which varied from one to the next, but to which men were elected or appointed locally by the provincials themselves. Sometimes, as we know was the case in Bithynia in Asia Minor, which Pompey set up as a province in the late 60s BC, some of the regulations about elections were laid down in the *lex provinciae*, but by and large the administration of local government remained a local affair. It was these officials within the cities who were responsible for the law in the region (especially in the 'allied' and 'free' cities) and for the maintenance of local amenities such as sewage, water-supply, etc. They in turn would rely on local rich men to provide improvements in these amenities out of their own pockets. A good example is provided by an inscription from Aletrium, in Italy, which proclaims that the local senate appointed one of its benefactors as superintendent of works, and that he paved the town's streets, built a portico, provided a playing field, a water-clock, a market, seats and a bathing pool; redecorated the town hall; and constructed a reservoir and an aqueduct [Dessau, *ILS* 5348]. Not surprisingly the local senate paid him and his son many honours in return. Although most provinces would not have benefactors on this scale, the inscription illustrates well the amount that could be done by private donations.

Coloniae and *municipia*

In addition to these non-Roman cities, the provinces also contained towns whose inhabitants were Roman citizens, known as *coloniae* and *municipia*, although there were few of them before the very end of the republic. *Coloniae* were originally military settlements, made up of veterans from the army, while *municipia* were already existing towns which gained the Roman citizenship, of which there were naturally a large number in Italy by Cicero's time. These functioned in the provinces much as did the allied cities, though their institutions were understandably much more like those of Rome itself than were those, say, of the Greek cities; and they had the immense additional advantage of Roman citizenship, which meant that governors had to be much more careful about how they treated them.

We can see that much of what we would consider to be the

normal day-to-day administration of the provinces was not the concern of the governor at all, especially during the republican period. His functions, based on his military command, were concentrated on a fairly small number of tasks compared with a modern administrator. This of course is what made it possible for a governor to carry on the government of his province, despite the fact that he had only a relatively small and relatively inexperienced team to help him.

Provincial administration: the governor's view

If in the official view provincial government was essentially a military matter, what of the attitudes of the men who were actually sent by the senate to carry out these tasks? Of course different individuals are bound to have had different opinions, but we do have enough clues to be able to see how at least some Romans faced the prospect.

The governor about whose own thoughts we know most is Cicero, because many of the letters he wrote have survived. It is quite clear that he detested the time he spent in Cilicia, from the moment the possibility first arose of his going there until his eventual return to Italy. His appointment came as a particularly unpleasant shock to Cicero because he had not gone to a province after his consulship in 63 BC. However, a law of Pompey's, passed in 52 BC, laid down that there should be a period of five years between magistracy and governorship. Pompey's law was probably aimed at preventing a man from standing for office and spending large sums on bribery in the process, in the hope of making good his losses at the expense of the provincials a year later. However, it also meant that the men who would previously have gone to the provinces immediately after their consulships or praetorships now had to wait, so that there was a temporary shortage of governors. As a result, men like Cicero, who had so far avoided the task, were called in to fill the gap. Cicero's letters are full of complaints. Even while he was in Athens, on his way out to his province, he wrote to his friend Atticus:

> How unsuited this business is to my way of life! How true is that proverb 'Each to his own task'! You will be saying, 'What? You haven't even got to work yet!' I know it, and believe me the worst is yet to come.   [Cicero, *Letters to Atticus* V 10.3]

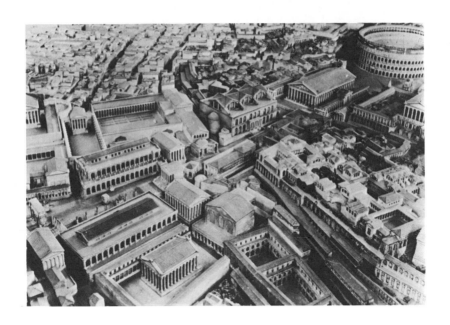

6   *A model of Rome, as it would have looked in the age of the emperors*

For Cicero it was absence from Rome that hurt most. He wrote later from a military encampment in Cilicia to his correspondent in Rome, Caelius Rufus:

> The city, the city, my dear Rufus! Hold fast to it and live in its light! All service abroad, as I decided from my youth, is mean and sordid for any one who can make a name for himself by working in Rome.   [Cicero, *Letters to his Friends* II 12.2]

As a result, he was for ever worrying that he would not be replaced promptly at the end of his year in the province and, at the earliest opportunity, left to come home, entrusting the care of the province to a young man whom he admitted to Atticus to be wholly unsuitable for the job.

It may be that Cicero's views were extreme, but it is quite likely that something of this dislike for provincial government affected many of his colleagues. After all, to men like Cicero and Verres, the governorship of a province was not something they had chosen because they especially wanted to do it; it was merely one stage in their political careers at Rome, and one which took them away from the centre of the political world, Rome itself.

One result of this was that the governor hoped to get from his term something that would be of benefit to him in his own political career in Rome. The two most obvious things were firstly military glory, and secondly money. The Greek historian Appian, writing in the mid-second century AD and looking back three hundred years to the second century BC, puts it neatly:

> There were some who sought from their governorships reputation, gain or the glory of a triumph and not the advantage of the Roman state. [Appian, *Iberika* 80.349]

So we find Cicero anxious to get full recognition for his success over the Cilician bandits at Pindinessus. On the other hand Verres, according to Cicero, boasted openly about how he was able to plunder his province; and how he was not keeping it all for himself but that

> he had divided up the three years of his governorship in Sicily, so that he would reckon he had done well if he could use the profits of one year for himself, hand over the second to his patrons and to his defenders (*at his trial*); and keep back the third, the most lucrative and profitable year, entirely to bribe the jury.
> [Cicero, *First Verrine* 14]

IGNORANCE AND APATHY AT ROME

One result of these attitudes was a marked lack of interest or concern for what went on in the provinces among politicians in Rome itself. As Cicero himself said in a speech he delivered some three years before he went to Cilicia, 'There is so much happening at Rome, that events in the provinces are hardly heard of.' He goes on to illustrate this with a story about his own career. As a young man he had been appointed as one of the two financial officers (*quaestores*) in Sicily, one of whom was based in Syracuse and the second (Cicero in this case) at the other end of the island in the port of Lilybaeum. At the end of his term of office, Cicero returned to Italy, proud of all he had achieved in Sicily and convinced that his quaestorship would be the talk of the town in Rome itself. He landed at the port and sea-side resort of Puteoli, where he met a man who, believing that he had just come from Rome, asked for the latest news.

When I answered that I had just left my province, he said, 'Why, of course. Africa, if I'm not mistaken.' By now I was pretty well furious. 'No, *Sicily*', I replied. Just then someone else appeared, acting the know-all. 'What! Don't you know?' he said. 'Our friend here has just come from being quaestor at *Syracuse*.' So what then? I gave up my anger, and became a holiday-maker, like all the others.

[Cicero, *For Plancius* 64–65]

But if the politicians in Rome were largely ignorant and apathetic about what was going on in the provinces overseas, it would be a mistake to think that they were simply callous and indifferent to the lot of the provincials, and prepared to allow the governors to exploit them as much as they liked. If this had been the case, then there was no reason why Verres, for example, should have been brought to trial at all. Nevertheless, there is no doubt that, in practice, protection was much more readily available to the relatively small number of rich and powerful men in the province who had personal connections of their own with individual Romans and their families. For example, Verres seems to have caused particular offence at Rome by his mistreatment of Sthenius, from the town of Thermae on the northern coast of the island, who had close relationships with many important Romans, including Cicero and Verres himself, and most importantly with Pompey. Men like Sthenius had strings to pull, and an appeal from one of them could bring results.

The Roman view of the provinces

The Romans' own view of their provinces and of their government of them was strongly influenced by two major factors, both of which were connected to the sort of men who were sent out as governors and the positions these men held within the Roman state. The governors were essentially the elected magistrates of the city of Rome itself and as such they were men in the middle of a political career, chosen to fulfil the judicial and military needs of the city itself. This left a strong imprint on the methods they used in governing their provinces and on the scope of the tasks they had to undertake, and the powers they could use to complete them. The position of the inhabitants of the provinces too was conditioned by these factors. To a considerable extent, they were left to run their own communities, but when, as inevitably happened,

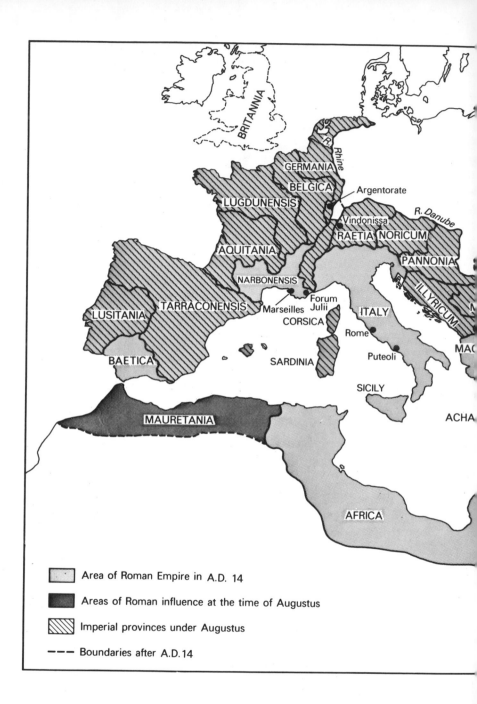

BRITANNIA

GERMANIA

BELGICA

Argentorate

LUGDUNENSIS

R. Danube

Vindonissa

RAETIA NORICUM

PANNONIA

AQUITANIA

ILLYRICUM

NARBONENSIS

Forum
Julii

TARRACONENSIS Marseilles

ITALY

LUSITANIA

CORSICA

Rome

MA(

BAETICA

SARDINIA

Puteoli

SICILY

ACHA

MAURETANIA

AFRICA

Area of Roman Empire in A.D. 14

Areas of Roman influence at the time of Augustus

Imperial provinces under Augustus

— — — Boundaries after A.D. 14

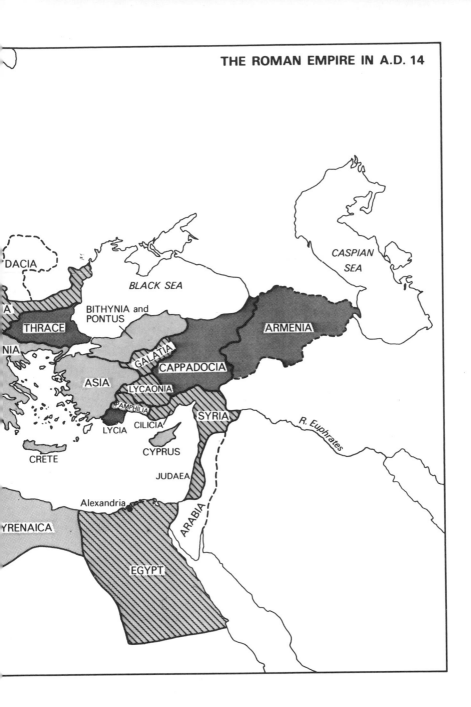

THE ROMAN EMPIRE IN A.D. 14

DACIA

BLACK SEA

CASPIAN SEA

A

BITHYNIA and
PONTUS

THRACE

ARMENIA

NIA

GALATIA

CAPPADOCIA

ASIA

LYCAONIA

PAMPHILIA

SYRIA

R. Euphrates

LYCIA

CILICIA

CYPRUS

CRETE

JUDAEA

Alexandria

ARABIA

YRENAICA

EGYPT

they came into collision with the wishes of the governor himself there was little they could do. Even the opportunities made available to them, through the courts in Rome for instance, were only of much use to the rich and powerful. But then the governor was the representative of the might of the Roman armies, and it is perhaps surprising that the provincials had even as much say in the matter as they did.

4

The empire and the emperors

THE revolution that led to the establishment of Augustus as emperor at Rome in 27 BC brought changes to the administration of the provinces, as it did to all other aspects of Roman political life. The emperor himself claimed, in the record of his own achievements:

> In my sixth and seventh consulships (28–27 BC), once I had put an end to the civil wars, when I was, with the agreement of all, in complete control of affairs, I transferred the state from my own power to the control of the senate and people of Rome.
>
> [*Res Gestae*, 34.1]

Although, shortly after, writers talk of his restoration of the old form of public affairs, the historian Tacitus, writing about one hundred years later, could say openly that the defeat of Marcus Antonius at Actium in 31 BC had placed all power in the hands of one man.

Tacitus also tells us that the provincials were optimistic about their prospects under the new regime:

> The provinces were not unfavourable to this state of affairs, for they had reason to suspect government by the senate and people, because of the conflicts between powerful politicians and the greed of the governors. The laws offered no protection when they could be overturned by force, favouritism and, finally, by money.
>
> [Tacitus, *Annals* I.2]

It is now a common view that they were not disappointed, and that Augustus' changes in the provincial system did bring an improvement from the republican system. Just how true this is we must see after we have looked at what Augustus actually did.

Augustus' changes in the government of the provinces

When in 27 BC Augustus laid down the extraordinary and unconstitutional powers that he had held during the struggle with Antonius, and handed over the control of the empire to the senate, neither he nor the senators can have been very surprised when a large section of it was given straight back to him. In effect he was appointed governor of the provinces of Gaul, most of Spain, Syria, Cilicia and Cyprus; and, when various new provinces were added, especially along the Danube frontier, these were entrusted to him as well. The remainder continued, as under the republic, to be governed by senatorial ex-magistrates.

The reasons why Augustus chose to control these provinces is fairly clear. These were the areas of the empire which required heavy concentrations of troops, either because they might be threatened from outside or because they were likely to be disturbed by unruly inhabitants from within. For these military reasons it was important that the governor should be able to stay in charge of his province for a reasonable length of time. As we saw in chapter 1, it was this situation which had led under the republic to the emergence of great army leaders who were in a position to threaten the state itself, and which made possible eventually the

7 *The beginning of the* Res Gestae – *Augustus' own record of his achievements – from an inscription at Ankara in Turkey*

establishment of the one-man rule of Augustus. It was a lesson which the emperor had learnt well, and he certainly did not want any other senatorial commanders to be in a position to threaten the state, now that he was firmly in control of it.

THE GOVERNORS OF AUGUSTUS' PROVINCES

However it was clearly quite impossible for Augustus to be governor of these vast areas of the known world in the same sense in which Cicero was pro-consul in Cilicia. To meet this problem he extended an institution already well known and understood under the republic. We have seen how Cicero and his contemporaries took with them experienced military men to act as lieutenants, or *legati*. Similarly Augustus appointed *legati* to act for him in the different provinces. But because they had to act more as a republican governor had done than as republican *legati*, they were granted a certain degree of independent power. Augustus himself, at least from 23 BC onwards, held the power (*imperium*) of a proconsul. To avoid difficulties with other provincial governors, who might also be proconsuls, Augustus' power was made superior to that of the ordinary proconsuls, and was termed 'greater *imperium*', or *imperium maius*. His subordinates were given the *imperium pro praetore*, showing that their power was less than that of the emperor, and that they were directly under his supervision. They held the title of *legati Augusti pro praetore*.

GOVERNORS FROM THE EQUESTRIAN ORDER

There was one other category of governor directly appointed by Augustus. These were the *praefecti* who were in charge in several small but awkward provinces, such as the frontier provinces of Raetia and Noricum on the Danube, and the area of Judaea, with its nationalist and religious problems for the Romans. (Pontius Pilate, for example, was prefect in Judaea in the reign of Tiberius.) Also the great province of Egypt, which Augustus had taken over on the death of the queen Cleopatra, after the death of Antonius, had a *praefectus* in charge. These men differed from the *legati Augusti* in that they were not senators, but members of the equestrian order. This meant that they were people of some wealth and standing in Roman society, but not members of senatorial families. The use of such men was a major change, for they were the first governors to come from outside the senate; but, as the military title of prefect suggests, they too can be considered essentially military men. With one exception, their provinces were small. The exception was of course Egypt, and the *praefectus Aegypti* was in many ways the most important governor in the Roman world. His superiority to the other *praefecti* was clear when later (probably in the reign of the emperor Claudius, AD 41-54) the minor prefects began to be called procurators, a term which, as we shall see, emphasised their direct dependence on the emperor himself; the great *praefectus Aegypti* however, though still appointed by the emperor, retained the title Augustus had given him. It was an office held only by equestrians of high standing, and usually at the end of their careers.

THE ORGANISATION OF FINANCES

Augustus' changes in the military balance of the empire brought major alterations to the government of at least some of the provinces. This change in personnel also meant some alteration to the governor's staff in the provinces which Augustus controlled directly (usually called the 'imperial', as opposed to the 'senatorial', provinces). Under the republic the governor's chief financial officer had been the *quaestor*, himself a junior elected magistrate. It would have been strange for a *legatus* to have a magistrate working under him; and in any case Augustus no doubt wanted to choose the financial supervisors of his own provinces more directly than would have been possible if he relied on men elected by the people of Rome. Therefore there appear in the imperial provinces men called *procuratores Augusti*, the imperial procurators – the same title as was later to be used by the equestrian governors of the minor provinces. The word *procurator* had previously meant someone employed as an agent, particularly by anyone who had to be away from Rome for a time on state business. These financial procurators were the emperor's own agents looking after financial affairs in the imperial provinces. Usually they too belonged to the equestrian order, although some of them were former imperial slaves. In any case, they were not senators, and this again marks a departure from the senate's monopoly in the field of provincial administration.

As might be expected, the emperor used financial agents of this sort for tasks other than the public finances of the imperial provinces. In particular he had acquired by various means a large amount of property which belonged previously to local rulers and other powerful men. This was not of course confined to the imperial

8   *Augustus – a cameo portrait*

provinces, and as a result procurators were regularly appointed to
superintend such properties throughout the empire. They were also
in a good position to let the emperor know what was happening in
the provinces in which they were based, and although they had no
official standing in the state hierarchy, they could be useful sources
of information.

THE SENATORIAL PROVINCES

However, despite the far-reaching effects that these changes were to
have on the way Rome administered her provinces, in theory the
situation was just as it had been under the republic. Augustus was a

proconsul who happened to have extraordinarily large powers. The point is reinforced by looking at what was happening in the senatorial provinces. There the powers of the governor and the composition of his staff were almost exactly the same as under the republic. Naturally there was much less emphasis on his military duties, since Augustus was deliberately trying to play these down; and to avoid a proconsul building up too powerful a hold over his province, the length of time he was there was shortened, and was often reduced to one year only. But the main difference, and it was a large one, was that now there was not only a senate at Rome of whose opinions the governor had to take note, but also the emperor.

THE CONTROLS ON THE GOVERNOR

There is no doubt that the changes in the provincial system which Augustus introduced gave the emperor far more direct control over his own *legati* and *praefecti* than had been exercised by the senate under the republic. Also, because of his specially increased *imperium* (*imperium maius*) and the simple fact that he was by far the most powerful man in the Roman world, he could, and occasionally did, intervene in provinces governed by proconsuls appointed by the senate.

But as we have seen under the republic, the interests of the provincials were not much helped by the mere fact that machinery existed to control bad governors, if that machinery was not properly used. Before we can decide if they were better off under the reign or principate, as it was called, of Augustus and his successors, we must see whether the controls Augustus had introduced were in fact operated to help the provincials.

The law which was used to check the activities of the provincial governor under the republic was the law on recovery of illegal gains – the *lex de repetundis*. This remained the basis of legal actions under the empire also, but there was one major change in the law. At least from the time of the emperor Tiberius (AD 14–37), important prosecutions were conducted not before a jury-court under a praetor as in the republic, but in the senate. Cases concerning equestrian officials were often heard by the emperor himself.

The difficulty is to know whether the provincials could get a fair hearing before either of these courts, any more than they could in the republican jury-courts. The real difficulty was that a deputation of provincials could only plead their case against a former governor to a senate composed of former governors. What was more, senators tended to consider criticism of themselves as an impertinence. Pliny, who as we shall see was himself involved in provincial affairs at the end of his life, and before that was a leading orator in Rome, commented that a leader of a deputation from Bithynia in Asia Minor damaged his case by presuming 'most impudently' to speak a second time, following two men of consular rank and eloquent men at that. Equally the emperor might well look to his own and the state's advantage rather than that of his subjects. Tiberius is said to have written to governors who were urging that burdensome taxes should be put on the provinces that 'it is the job of a good shepherd to shear his flock, not to skin it' [Suetonius, *Life of Tiberius* 32]. This shows that he was not encouraging extortionate demands, but only to avoid being unable to draw more revenue later. Worse still was Augustus' handling of the case of a procurator of Gaul. This man, Licinus, was a Gaul himself, and had been an imperial slave. When put in charge of the finances of his native country, he proceeded to extort enormous sums from the provincials by blatant frauds. When the Gauls complained to Augustus, Licinus handed over a vast amount of treasure to the emperor, saying that he had collected it for the benefit of the emperor and the people of Rome, and was promptly acquitted. This could have brought little comfort to the wretched Gauls.

In many ways then the situation was not as different for the provincials under the principate as we might imagine. In particular it remained almost impossible to get rid of a governor while he was still in charge of his province. The Jewish writer Philo, who lived in Alexandria under the emperor Gaius (AD 37–41), described the situation like this:

> Some of those who were provincial governors perverted their charge as guardian and protector into dominion and tyranny, and spread misery through their provinces with their corruption, robbery, injustice, expulsion and banishment of the innocent, and the execution of important men without trial. But these people were required by the emperor to render an account on their return to Rome after ending their term of office. [Philo, *Against Flaccus* 105]

But, as Philo goes on to stress, these trials always took place *after* completion of their period in the province. He warmly praises Augustus and Tiberius for punishing bad governors after they

IMP·CAESAR·DIVI·F·
AVGVSTVS
PONTIFEX·MAXIMVS
IMP·XII·COS·XI·TRIB·POT·XIV·
AEGVPTO·IN·POTESTATEM
POPVLI·ROMANI·REDACTA·
SOLI·DONVM·DEDIT·

9   *An Egyptian obelisk brought to Rome by Augustus – a symbol of Rome's world-wide power*

had left their provinces, but also says that he knew of no example in their reigns of one who had been removed from office to stand trial.

It seems that the main reason for the controls on provincial officials which Augustus introduced, was the need for a close watch to be kept on men holding substantial military power. There is no sign that the intention was to improve the lot of the provincials, nor much to show that, from the point of view of relations with the Roman governors, it did improve.

The principate: the governed and the governors

In some ways however life *was* much improved. The provinces had suffered just as much as the Romans themselves from the civil wars fought over their territory, which led to the establishment of Augustus as *princeps*. The peace which followed, and which was in part a result of the new arrangements Augustus made for the governing of the provinces, meant that the provincials could lead their lives in relative security, and in this atmosphere the cities of the provinces became prosperous.

THE PROVINCIAL ASSEMBLIES

One result of this was the great increase in building, especially of grand public buildings such as baths, amphitheatres and town halls, and considerable pride in the local community. The rich and powerful in the cities were both able and happy to adorn them to an extent unknown under the republic. This local feeling strengthened the importance of another institution, the provincial representative assembly, usually called the *concilium* in the Western provinces or the *koinon* in the Greek-speaking East. If a complaint was lodged against a governor, or a vote of thanks made in his favour, it often came from this body, although it is clear from several examples that a clever governor could win over a few important members of the assembly and thus effectively control their decisions. One rich provincial, Claudius Timarchus from Crete

> said on several occasions that it was in his power to determine whether the proconsuls who governed Crete received their vote of thanks. [Tacitus, *Annals* XV 20]

ROMAN CITIZENSHIP

There was another change slowly taking place which did affect the freedom of the governor, and that was the increase in the number of Roman citizens in the provinces. Not only were new *coloniae* and *municipia* being established, but grants of citizenship were made to individuals among the provincial population who had been of assistance to Rome. These were usually the great men of the area, who had considerable influence on the provincial communities. They were clearly people whom the governor would beware of antagonising in any case, and the additional advantage of the citizenship gave them not only prestige, but privileges under Roman law.

INCREASED CONCERN AT ROME

Despite the short-comings of the governors and the lack of interest shown by the emperor in controlling them, life in the provinces probably improved during the early years of the principate. Moreover, the emperor was not deaf to appeals for help from particular provincial communities. When an earthquake struck the cities of the province of Asia, Augustus provided funds for restoration. At another level the same emperor was prepared to listen sympathetically to an embassy from the city of Cnidos in Asia, asking for an investigation of a murder case, and to write to the proconsul of Asia, instructing him to look into it. But again, as under the republic, the initiative for intervention had to come from the provinces themselves. The new government in Rome did not feel duty-bound to look after the interests of the provincials, any more than the old one had.

There was one other factor which had changed since the days of the republic, which was bound to transform slowly the way in which the provinces were administered. Under the republic a governor's term in his province had been a necessary but, for many, unwelcome time away from the real business of life – governing Rome and her empire from the senate of Rome itself. Once the real power had been transferred from the senate to one man, the emperor, this could no longer be the case. Although the senate was always supplied by the emperor with matters to debate, and though the old forms and traditions were kept up by the senators, the real control of events now lay with the emperor himself, and the real work of governing the Roman world was done by those in the emperor's service. For a man involved in public life this was bound to give more interest and importance to the tasks that the emperor allotted, including the administration of the provinces.

Along with this went a gradual increase of concern at Rome with the way the provinces ran themselves, not only from the military point of view, which had dominated the republic and the first years of the principate, but with the internal affairs of the provincial communities themselves, which earlier Romans had been happy to leave well alone. This can be seen partly in the encouragement given to the provincials to found cities of their own, with institutions often modelled on Roman lines, which led to the appearance of flourishing towns in areas that had previously no tradition of urban development, such as Britain and, more especially, Gaul; and partly in the appointment of special commissioners from time to time to look into the affairs of the long-established cities of the eastern provinces. So began the process which was to produce eventually an immensely complicated bureaucratic system of governmental control in the last centuries of the Roman empire. Certainly the provinces were gradually receiving more and more government from Rome itself. The question which remains is, were they receiving *better* government?

5

Two imperial governors:
Agricola and Pliny the Younger

PROBABLY the easiest way to see the effects of the changes that took place in the early empire is to look briefly at the careers of two men of whom we happen to know a good deal, and who were both involved in provincial administration.

Agricola in Britain, AD 78–84

Gnaeus Julius Agricola was governor of the imperial province of Britain from AD 78 to 84, an unusually long period at that time. We know more about his term in his province than those of most governors because his biography was written after his death by his son-in-law, the historian Tacitus. Not surprisingly, the picture Tacitus gives is wholly favourable, and there is at least the suspicion that he has exaggerated his father-in-law's achievements, and played down the work done by his predecessors in Britain. Nevertheless the biography does shed much light both on the Roman conquest of Britain, and on the work of its governors at this period.

AGRICOLA'S BACKGROUND

Agricola was himself a provincial, born in the *colonia* of Forum Iulii (modern Fréjus) in southern Gaul. Both his grandfathers had held the Roman citizenship, and had been imperial procurators. His father had advanced further up the social and political hierarchy, and had been an active member of the Roman senate, until he had fallen out of favour with the emperor Gaius (AD 37–41). Agricola himself had gone through the traditional list of magistracies still necessary for a senator, which led to his holding the consulship for part of the year in AD 77. By that time he had already served

ROMAN BRITAIN

? Mons Graupius

CALEDONIA

Antonine Wall

Hadrian's Wall

Mona
(Anglesey)

Eburacum
(York)

BRITANNIA

Deva
(Chester)

Verulamium
(St Albans)

Londinium
(London)

twice in Britain, once as military tribune (a junior officer grade), and later, after his praetorship in AD 68, as commander of one of the four legions stationed in the island. Thus when the emperor Vespasian chose him to be *legatus Augusti pro praetore* in Britain from 78, he already had considerable knowledge both of military affairs and of conditions in Britain itself.

Britain needed a military man with experience of the local situation more than did most provinces. The conquest which had begun under the emperor Claudius in AD 42 was far from complete, and when Agricola arrived he had still to finish off the subjugation of north Wales by the capture of the island of Mona (Anglesey), and also to consolidate the work of his predecessors with raids and the building of forts in the north of England. After this he spent his last four campaigning seasons in the province extending Roman control into southern Scotland and to the edge of the central Highlands, north of Perth.

Although the details of Agricola's campaigns do not concern us here, it is clear from Tacitus' account that the main task facing the governor of Britain was to subdue and pacify the unruly tribes that inhabited the island, and to extend the Roman province by force of arms. By far the greatest part of Agricola's time was taken up with the command of the Roman army in the field, and it was clearly with this in mind that the emperor had chosen a man with Agricola's especial abilities and knowledge.

AGRICOLA IN BRITAIN: CIVILIAN MATTERS

Yet even in the midst of this campaigning, the governor had civilian matters to attend to. At the end of his first year in Britain, Agricola turned his attention to the administration of the province, taking care, as Tacitus tells us, to appoint honourable men, and to restrict the expenditure of his own household (just as Cicero had done). He found that, in the matter of the collection of corn and of tribute, exactly the same sort of abuses were being practised by provincial officials as had been done by Verres in Sicily in the days of the republic. These he cut out, thus making the system fairer and more bearable. The reason Tacitus gives for his doing this is interesting:

> He understood the feelings of the province and had learnt from the experience of others that military success was of little use if it was followed by injustices; so he decided to root out the causes of wars. . . . By suppressing these abuses in his first year he gave a good reputation to peace, which from the negligence or arrogance of his predecessors had been feared as much as war.
>
> [Tacitus, *Agricola* 19.1 and 20.1]

Though Tacitus may as usual be being too kind to Agricola and too severe on his predecessors, it is clear that not all imperial legates were ideal provincial governors. It is important to notice also that even Agricola's enlightened approach stemmed from the realisation that the Britons would give him less trouble if handled reasonably.

At the end of the next campaigning season, Agricola's civilian policy went into full swing. He helped the Britons to build towns on the Roman model with temples, a forum and private houses. The sons of native rulers were given a Roman education, and the use of the Latin language was encouraged. Even Roman styles of dress were adopted by native Britons. Tacitus sees all this in a somewhat cynical light:

> Little by little they were led astray by the attraction of evil ways, colonnades, baths and elegant banquets. The ignorant called this civilisation; in fact it was a part of their slavery.
>
> [Tacitus, *Agricola*, 21.3]

Archaeological evidence confirms Tacitus' account of the Roman policy of town-building, if not the interpretation he places upon it. Several Romano-British towns were laid out in the last decades of the first century AD, and at one in particular, Verulamium (modern St Albans), an inscription survives which was put up at the entrance to the newly-built forum in the year AD 79, during Agricola's governorship.

Agricola's governorship in Britain tells us much about provincial administration at the time. Two points are especially worth noticing. Firstly, it is clear that in some things the situation had not changed much since the days of the republic. In this province at least military matters were the governor's chief preoccupation, and like his equivalent under the republic, he seems to have had large powers in the fields of administration and justice. Equally Agricola's predecessors, even if not Agricola himself, had indulged in or permitted the same sort of extortion and fraud on the provincials that some republican governors had committed. On the other hand, and this is the second point, Agricola's appointment and success do illustrate one of the advantages of the system Augustus had introduced. Agricola was clearly a specialist where Britain was concerned, and was particularly well-fitted by his own provincial background and his experience in the island itself for the task he had to perform. This sort of selection was simply

10　*A monument to Julius Classicianus, an imperial procurator in Britain (shortly before Agricola's governorship). He was probably born in north-east Gaul.*

impossible under the republican system, where the province was assigned its governor by a deliberately haphazard process. Under the principate the government of the provinces is seen less as a political prize, or as a step in a career based in the Roman senate, and more as a job that needed to be carried out by men with particular skills and experience.

Pliny in Bithynia-Pontus, AD 110–113

Another Roman of this period whose time in a province is particularly well-known to us is Gaius Plinius Caecilius Secundus, usually called Pliny the Younger, to distinguish him from his uncle, the Elder Pliny, some of whose writings have also survived.

PLINY'S BACKGROUND

Pliny in fact was never a provincial governor in the ordinary sense. He had followed a normal and successful senatorial career, and was also successful as a pleader in the courts. Twice he was given positions in the central imperial administration connected with finance, once from AD 96 to 98 under the emperor Domitian at the military treasury, which looked after the retirement pay of veterans in the army, and once, from AD 98 to 100, under the emperor Trajan at the *aerarium Saturni,* which was concerned with more general matters of state finance. He was therefore a man with considerable legal and financial expertise, and well-equipped for the task Trajan eventually gave him.

PLINY'S TASK IN BITHYNIA-PONTUS

In AD 110 the emperor appointed Pliny to go to the province of Bithynia-Pontus (see map p. 43) as a *legatus pro praetore* with consular powers. The oddity of this was that normally Bithynia was one of the provinces governed not by an imperial legate, but by a proconsul drawn from the senate. The letters which Pliny wrote back to the emperor, and Trajan's replies, have survived in the collection of Pliny's letters to his friends, and it is clear from these that there was reason to be worried about the financial and political state of the province. There had been signs of dissatisfaction with their governors by the provincials, and in the ten years before he was sent to the province, Pliny himself had undertaken the defence of two governors of Bithynia, prosecuted under the *lex de repetundis* for allegedly making illegal gains. Clearly all was not well with Bithynia, whether because of bad administration by the governors or the excessive hostility of some of the local provincials, and this alone might explain why a *legatus pro praetore* whom the emperor could choose was sent to the province. It would also explain the addition of the powers of a consul, which ordinary imperial governors did not have.

PLINY IN HIS PROVINCE

Pliny's letters show that his task was not concerned with the usual functions of a governor, such as jurisdiction and maintenance of law and order on a day-to-day basis, but with the overhauling of the institutions of the cities in the province, as well as with certain abuses of the provincial system there. Because of this he spent much of his time examining the accounts and regulating the business of the local town-councils. He had of course to take care not to ignore the special status of the two 'free' cities of the province, and of the two Roman *coloniae.* For example, he enforced throughout the province a decision of Trajan banning assemblies of provincials, for fear that they would take on a political character that would disturb the peace of the province. Thus he forbade meetings as different as those of the Christians and of the fire

11 *An aqueduct at Segovia, in central Spain, built in the first century* AD, *and still in use*

brigade in the city of Nicomedia. However when the 'free and allied' city of Amisus handed him a petition about their local benefit-society, formed as a club for the poorer citizens, he wrote for advice to the emperor, and received the following reply:

Trajan to Pliny. If the citizens of Amisus, whose petition you enclosed, are permitted to have a benefit-society by their own laws, which they use under the provisions of a treaty, we ought not interfere with them, especially if the money they collect is used not for riotous and illegal meetings, but to assist cases of hardship among the poor. In the other cities, which are subject to our law, institutions of this kind must be prohibited.   [Pliny, *Letters* X 93]

Clearly Trajan too is more influenced by the status of the city than the needs of the poor, as there must have been many poor citizens in communities which did not have a treaty.

Pliny also had to deal with some matters which showed that his predecessors in the province had not been as careful as they ought to have been. A number of letters about the imperial postal system indicate that abuses may have been practised in the past, perhaps by officials who could sell illegal permits to use it. Pliny also found that a number of slaves had been recruited into the army, probably as substitutes for men who wanted to avoid conscription. Again, he found some men, who had been condemned to the mines for various misdeeds, working as town officials, allegedly on the order of previous governors. We can understand Trajan's reply:

Let us remember that the reason for sending you to the province was that much clearly needed to be reformed.   [Pliny, *Letters* X 32]

The investigation that took up most of Pliny's time was into the finances of the cities themselves. These provincial communities seem to have been extremely prosperous, so much so that they were indulging in wasteful and foolish expense. One instance will illustrate the point. Nicomedia, the capital of the Roman province, needed a water supply. Pliny describes to Trajan the steps that they took:

The inhabitants of Nicomedia, Sir, have spent 3,318,000 sesterces on an aqueduct, which was abandoned before it was finished, and eventually pulled down. They then made a grant of 200,000 sesterces towards another. This also has been abandoned, so that if they are to have water, they must spend still more, even after having wasted such a vast sum.   [Pliny, *Letters* X 37]

This is a particularly bad example of what Pliny found in many of the cities of the province.

It is interesting to see that the emperor was sufficiently worried about the affairs of the cities in Bithynia to send out a special governor to put them right. Moreover the man he chose was clearly an expert in the fields of law and finance which he would have to investigate. Once again we can see how a certain professionalism was being introduced into the administration of the provinces through the direct intervention of the emperor, even if many of Pliny's predecessors were much more like the amateur administrators who had governed the provinces of the republic. It was now important to Rome that the provincials should be efficiently organised, even if this meant altering the way in which the governor was appointed, and interfering much more directly with the self-government of the cities of the provinces. Even if, as is probable, Pliny died in his province before he could finish the task he had been given, he had brought about many changes in the way the province was governed, and, more importantly, in the way the provincials managed their own affairs.

6

Conclusion

THE size and endurance of the Roman empire was the single most remarkable achievement of the Roman people. We have seen now some of the ways in which Roman rule worked in the provinces, but it is worth while pausing to think about just what the Romans were trying to do through their control of the provinces, and what effect this had on the course of history.

The Roman empire: two views

Although Roman writers did not often comment at length on the reasons for their empire or its success, here are two radically different versions which have come down to us. The first is given by Vergil, the greatest of the poets living in the reign of the emperor Augustus. In his poem on the arrival in Italy of the Trojans who, according to legend, were the founders of the Roman race, his hero Aeneas visits the land of the dead, where his father describes to him the glories of the city which will eventually be built by his people. In a famous passage, he compares the greatness of the Romans with the artistic achievements of the Greeks:

> Others will, so I believe, beat out of bronze with greater delicacy creatures full of the breath of life, coax living features from marble, plead cases more expertly, plot and describe the movements of the sky and the rising of the stars. Remember, Roman, that your skill is to rule the nations with your power, to impose on them the ways of peace, to spare the conquered and by war to defeat the proud.
>
> [Vergil, *Aeneid* VI, 847–853][1]

These words are perhaps the noblest expression of the task of imperial Rome, as seen by a poet who lived through the last years

[1] See also R. D. Williams, *Aeneas and the Roman Hero* in this series.

of the republic and into the early years of the empire. In strong contrast is a view which Tacitus gives to Calgacus, a chieftain from Caledonia (modern Scotland), about to lead his people in a last desperate and unsuccessful battle against Agricola. This is how he describes the Romans:

> They are the plunderers of the world; once there is no more land left for their total devastation, they scour the sea as well. If their enemy is rich, they are greedy for wealth; if poor, they thirst for glory, so that neither the East nor the West will satisfy them. They alone out of the whole world lust after riches and poverty with equal passion. To robbery, slaughter and plunder they give the false name of 'empire'; they make a desert, and call it 'peace'.
>
> [Tacitus, *Agricola* 30]

The ideas which Tacitus gives to Calgacus here are clearly as biased against the Romans as those of Vergil are favourable. Yet in many ways the similarity of the picture given by the two passages is as marked as their differences. For both authors, the driving force behind the Roman empire was a desire to control the world, basically by force of arms, whether this is described as the 'plunder of the world' or as 'defeating the proud'.

EMPIRES ANCIENT AND MODERN

Although it might seem obvious that the Romans were interested in spreading their power and influence, this does in many ways separate their idea of empire from that of many more modern states. Thus although straightforward imperialism of this sort was no doubt present in the minds, for example, of the men who established the British empire in the nineteenth century, there were other important and publicly acknowledged factors as well. The trade, especially in raw materials, which Britain drew from her empire was of crucial importance, and so, to many Victorians, was the extension of the Christian religion to areas that had not received it. This type of consideration did not have nearly as much weight in the minds of the ancient Romans. To them the dominant idea was the enlarging of Rome's influence and control, and this inevitably meant military control.

Of course this did not exclude taking some thought for the welfare of the provincials. As Agricola saw, it was easier to main-

12 *Gemma Augustea: Part of a cameo, showing Augustus enthroned beside the goddess Roma (Rome), being crowned by Oikoumene (the inhabited world)*

tain even military control over people who were reasonably satisfied with their rulers, than over a discontented and potentially rebellious population. It did mean, though, that improving conditions in the provinces was always subordinated to the idea of holding them down with armed force ('sparing the conquered and by war defeating the proud', as Vergil puts it), and often put into practice by military men like Agricola himself.

The governors

If this overriding idea was present throughout the period we have been looking at, the outlook of the men who were sent to the provinces to carry it out does seem to have altered slowly, once Augustus had established one-man rule in Rome itself. Because of the great powers wielded by a governor, even when there was an emperor in Rome, this had a noticeable effect on the way in which the provinces were administered.

MORE GOVERNORS WITH SPECIAL SKILLS

The first change has already been noticed in the last two chapters, and is well illustrated by the governorships of Agricola and Pliny.

The fact that the emperor could choose men with special expertise to go to some at least of the provinces (normally those he controlled directly himself) meant that to some governors, their time in the provinces was less an unwelcome interruption in a senatorial career, and more a task to which they had been especially assigned by the emperor. At the same time the much smaller importance of the senate, once the emperor was in charge, may have reduced some of the exploitation of the financial and military position in which a republican governor had indulged in order to help his future career in the senate. Of course the emperor could not root out the temptation that was always present for governors to use their powers for their own profit, and the indications are that he did not always try very hard; but the changed situation in Rome is likely to have had some effect on the men who ruled in the provinces.

GOVERNORS FROM THE PROVINCES

There was one other gradual change which will have made a considerable difference to the morale of the provincials and which may have affected the outlook of the governors too. Unlike some more recent empires, Rome did not make a sharp distinction between those provincials to whom the Roman citizenship had been granted and those citizens who were natives of Italy. It was quite possible for men from the provinces themselves to become members of the Roman senate, and so to become in turn governors of the provinces. This was not a rapid process, and probably only applied to a small number of men when compared to the population of the empire as a whole. However, as we have seen, Agricola is one example of a man from the province of Gallia Narbonensis who became a provincial governor, and by the end of the first century, a man born in a province had already become emperor: Trajan (emperor from AD 98 to 117) came from Italica in southern Spain.

As a result of their involvement in the government of the Roman empire, the provincials are likely to have felt much more a part of the empire and less subjects of it. On the Roman side, it explains to some extent the increasing interest in the way in which the provinces administered themselves that we have seen in the case of Pliny's governorship in Bithynia-Pontus. Though this was inevitably a slow process, and one which had only just started in the period we have been examining, it was to lead eventually to a situation where, under the emperor Diocletian at the end of the third century AD, Rome was no longer the seat of the emperor of the Roman empire, and even Italy could be treated as two provinces.

The Roman empire: its achievement

To return to the place from which we began, the most striking and most important fact about the Roman empire was that it existed at all, and for such a long period. By the time the western part of the empire disappeared, broken into a series of barbarian kingdoms by the tribes which had invaded from Germany and central Europe, the Romans had ruled North Africa, the Near East, Asia Minor and the whole of western and southern Europe for more than four and a half centuries. From the accession of Augustus to the deposition of the last emperor in Italy is a period roughly equivalent to that from the time of the Wars of the Roses to the reign of Elizabeth II in England. That of itself is a military and political achievement unequalled in the history of the western world.

The effects of this achievement were not, however, just military and political. The stability of the empire over such a length of time meant that many of the ideas and institutions that existed in the days of the Romans are absolutely basic to the life we lead today. The literature and the philosophy of Greece, the legal system of Rome, the Christian religion are all part of the foundations of modern civilisation. It is not too much to say that it is because of the immense impact of the Roman empire that these ideas have survived to our day at all, let alone become so deeply embedded in our everyday life. The Roman empire itself was in turn the achievement of the men who conquered, ruled and administered the Roman provinces throughout those long centuries.

Appendix

Glossary of some technical terms used

aedile One of the city magistrates of Rome. As the minimum age at which a Roman politician could become an aedile was 37, it was often held between the quaestorship and the praetorship (see below) although, unlike those two magistracies, it was not an essential part of the *cursus honorum* (see below). The aedile was responsible for the general upkeep of the city itself – law and order, sanitation etc. – and also put on games for the people.

apparitores This was the general term for the minor civil servants that the governor took with him to his province – the heralds, messengers, door-keepers, clerks, etc.

client kings A modern term to describe the rulers of states which were under Roman protection but not Roman provinces. They were responsible for ruling their own kingdoms, and received support from the Romans, so long as they looked after Roman interests and followed Roman policy. They provided a useful means by which the senate could control various areas without having to send out a governor with a military force.

consul The two consuls, elected each year by the people, were the chief magistrates of the Roman state. For a Roman politician, the consulship represented the peak of his political career. They were responsible not only for the formulation of domestic policy, but were also the chief military commanders and, during and immediately after their term of office, would usually be put in charge of an important province.

cursus honorum The 'ladder of magistracies' which a Roman politician had to ascend in order to hold the various positions of power in the state. The offices in the *cursus* were the quaestorship, which could not be held before the age of 30, the praetorship (minimum age, 40) and the consulship (minimum age, 43).

equites These men, who formed the 'equestrian order', made up a class in the Roman state, defined by the amount of wealth they held (they had to possess 400,000 sesterces of property). They were distinguished from the senatorial class under the republic by the fact that they did not have a political career and thus did not enter the senate.

Most of them were probably landowners, but some undertook business on behalf of the state, which was prohibited to senators, and were called the *publicani* (see below). Under the empire some of these men were used in the provinces either as *praefecti* or *procuratores* (see below).

imperium The power given by the state to the magistrates (especially consuls and praetors), and, in particular, the power to command armies.

legati Under the republic the *legati* were sent out by the senate as senior assistants to army commanders and provincial governors, and often had special skills to help their superiors with their particular tasks. Under the empire the emperor sent *legati Augusti* to take charge of his own provinces.

praefectus A title given to some governors, drawn from the equestrian order (see *equites* above), and sent by the emperors to provinces directly under their control. Eventually most such governors became known as procurators (see below), and only the equestrian governor of Egypt retained the title of *praefectus*.

praetor One of the city magistrates of Rome, and an office on the *cursus honorum* (see above). The praetors were often put in charge of one of the law courts in Rome during their year of office. They were also sent, usually immediately after their period of office, to govern a province. The minimum age at which the praetorship could be held was 40.

proconsul and *propraetor* These were terms used to indicate that a man held the *imperium* (see above) of a consul or praetor, although at the time he was not holding either office. Often such men had just completed their period of office as consul or praetor. Proconsuls and propraetors were used as governors of provinces during the republic; under the empire the governors of 'senatorial' provinces held the title of proconsul.

procurator The word means 'agent'. The imperial procurators (*procuratores Augusti*) were used by the emperors for various purposes in the provinces. In particular they took care of financial matters in the emperor's own provinces, and of his financial interests in the 'senatorial' provinces. The term was also used for some governors of small provinces directly administered by the emperor, although under Augustus and Tiberius they had been called prefects (*praefecti*, see above). The procurators were usually men of the equestrian class (see *equites* above), although some were ex-slaves.

publicani These were members of the equestrian class (see *equites* above) who, during the republican period, formed themselves into companies to undertake public works for the state. These included building aqueducts, providing equipment and food for the army and collecting taxes. This last task made them important in the provinces.

quaestor A junior magistracy at Rome, and the first step on the *cursus honorum* (see above). From the time of Sulla's dictatorship (82–79 BC) a man elected to the quaestorship immediately became a senator. The minimum age for this office was 30. The tasks of a quaestor were mainly financial, and a quaestor would accompany a governor to his province to act as financial secretary.

scriba One of the most important minor civil servants (*apparitores*, see above) who accompanied a governor. He acted as chief clerk, and head of the governor's secretariat.

senate Although in theory the senate was merely a body to advise the consuls (see above), it became during the republic the ruling organ of the state. It consisted of people who had held magistracies already, and thus under the republic all provincial governors were already members of the senate. Even under the empire, when its powers were reduced because of the great importance of the emperor, it was still in theory responsible for all the provinces, and in practice appointed governors to a number of them (the so-called 'senatorial' provinces).

Index

Note: Roman provinces appear in bold type (e.g. **Achaea***)*